THE
CAMPER'S
POCKET
BOOK

NION

- Thought you might enjoy
this book in the
"wilderness"! Love ya
K

THE CAMPER'S POCKET HANDBOOK

A BACKCOUNTRY TRAVELER'S COMPANION

BY JOHN GOLL
EDITED BY HARRY ROBERTS

The Globe Pequot Press

Old Saybrook, Connecticut

Copyright © 1992 John Goll

Cover and text design by Casey Shain

Library of Congress Cataloging-in-Publication Data
Goll, John.
The camper's pocket handbook: a backcountry traveler's companion / by John Goll.
p. cm.
Includes index.
ISBN 0-7627-0423-3
1. Camping—Handbooks, manuals, etc. 2. Wilderness survival—Handbooks, manuals, etc.
I. Title
GV191.7.G65 1992   91-38414
796.54—dc20   CIP

Printed in Quebec, Canada
Revised Edition/First Printing

CONTENTS

ABOUT THE AUTHOR

John Goll is a businessman and veteran backcountry traveler having hiked and canoed the remote areas of North America for more than 30 years. He has completed several extensive solo Canadian canoe trips on rivers such as the Missinaibi, the Harricanaw and the Clearwater. John is the author of *Indiana State Parks*, a guidebook published by Glovebox Guidebooks of America.

ABOUT THE EDITOR

Harry Roberts, author of several popular books on outdoor recreation, is fondly remembered as "Uncle Harry" for his friendly writing style.

"THANKS"

I would like to extend my thanks to the following people for their support and assistance in making this book a reality:

To "Uncle Harry" Roberts, for his editing, rewriting, and the gift of his inimitable, easy reading style. To Dr. William Forgey, who helped plant the seed for this book and believed in it from the beginning. To Cliff Jacobson, for encouraging me along the way, and Tom Todd, for guiding me in developing the finished product. To Pete Brewster for his assistance in research for the evacuation and rescue chapter. And finally, to my daughter Amber Lynn, my boss and fellow backcountry traveler Paul Smith, and the Aid Company, Inc., for constant support and understanding when this book took too much of my time.

DEDICATION

To my father, who introduced
me to the backcountry.

HOW TO USE THIS BOOK

In spite of our best intentions and desires, very few of us manage to spend as much time in the wild as we want to. Unlike the explorers, voyageurs, and mountain men of the past, we're seldom able to live long enough in the wild, or go back often enough, to become as proficient in the skills of wilderness living as we are in the skills of surviving in civilization. We don't have a grizzly in the kitchen every day—but Jim Bridger never had to cope with the I-465 loop around Indianapolis either.

We read a great deal. We study the techniques and teachings of wilderness experts. But there's still an inescapable gap between the knowledge and skills we've studied, and the natural, automatic execution of those skills that comes only with extended practice for days, weeks, and months at a time. *The Camper's Pocket Handbook* will help you bridge that gap. It can do this only if you take it with you.

This book is small, light, and designed to be carried in the wild. There's little explanation of the "whys" behind the methods described and minimal discussion of recommended equipment.

Since this book is meant to be used in the wild, it wouldn't be very useful to take up space describing the latest in high-tech gear that you could have brought with you but didn't. Likewise, we'll tell you little more than just the essential points that you must remember to accomplish the task at hand.

All of our suggestions and techniques are based on the assumptions that you are reading this book in the midst of the wilderness, that you have an understanding of basic camping and outdoor skills, and that you are at least equipped with the "ten essentials." The "ten essentials" are briefly described in the first chapter and include the most basic pieces of equipment for wilderness living.

For equipment recommendations and detailed explanations of wilderness living skills, study the many fine books currently on the market. Those are the places to learn the basics in preparation for your trip. Then, when you're in the wild, look to this book for reminders and hints about putting the things you've already learned into practice.

This book fits your pocket or your pack, not your bookshelf. Take it to the wilderness, read it, refer to it, and use it to help you stay safe, healthy, and comfortable in the great outdoors. Use it to help you to attain what should be the ultimate goal of every wilderness experience—to enjoy it enough to go back and do it again.

MiND GAMES

Most of us who like to wander around in the outback are, to a greater or lesser extent, tech-weenies. We like the tools of the trade. There's something honest, functional, and clean about them. We stroke them and cluck over them.

And we frequently confuse our tools with knowledge!

Tools aren't knowledge. The best compass in the world is no better a tool for route-finding than the person using it. The lightest graphite paddle in the world is no better than a snow shovel in the hands of an inept paddler. The most important piece of gear you carry with you is your brain—and an empty brain is as useful as an empty water bottle in the deserts of the Anza-Borrego Wilderness.

But there's this curious paradox operating as well. Knowing something well and truly is valuable. But it will neither increase your pleasure or save your neck if your mind's in the wrong place. And wrong places of the mind abound. Fear is a wrong place. Macho is a wrong place. Conquest is a wrong place. All of these shut down your perceptions and keep you from seeing what's really out there. If you're consumed with fear about snakes dropping out of the trees into your canoe, you won't see the rock in the river. If you're hell-bent on showing your companions that you're the Ultimate Backcountry Animal, you'll probably need all the first aid skills you can get. And if all you're concerned with is adding one more notch on your hipbelt for yet another peak bagged or river run, you've missed the point entirely.

Old Nesmuk said it best, back around the turn of the century. "We don't go into the woods to rough it. We go to smooth it. We get it rough enough in town." Smoothing it isn't just a function of the latest and lightest high-tech gear. It's an easy, relaxed mind and a field of vision that includes all the world around you that smooths it for you—and your companions. It keeps you out of trouble, mostly. It keeps you calm and aware if trouble rears up and bites you in the ankle.

And it permits you to do what prompted you to venture into the outback in the first place, have a good time!

Relax friends. Nature isn't The Enemy. Wrong-headedness is.

—*Uncle Harry*

The Camper's Pocket Handbook

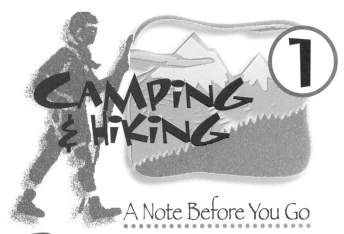

CAMPING & HIKING

1

A Note Before You Go

Before you depart on your trip to the back-country, remember to leave word with a contact person or agency who will be responsible for starting search and rescue procedures if you fail to check in by a deadline date and time. The law enforcement agency with jurisdiction over the area you will be in is usually best since it is readily available and has the authority and the resources for a search and rescue operation.

Be sure you tell your contacts your planned route, activities, and final deadline after which they should come looking for you. It is a good idea to allow yourself a day or so of leeway in case you are delayed by weather or other non-critical problems.

Finally, and most important, **DO NOT FAIL TO CHECK IN WITH YOUR CONTACTS AT THE END OF YOUR TRIP!** If you don't contact them, a great deal of time, effort, and money (possibly yours) will be spent looking for you while you are relaxing at home.

CAMPING & HIKING

When you're in the backcountry, you're a visitor in another world. It is a world where plants, animals and natural things have grown and lived in balance for thousands of years. You will have some impact on that fragile environment just by being there. Just how damaging and how lasting your impact is, however, is something you can control.

Remember; we didn't inherit our wilderness areas from our ancestors. They're on loan to us from our children.

THE TEN ESSENTIALS

In the 1930s the Seattle Mountaineers developed a list called the "Ten Essentials," the most important pieces of equipment that should be carried on any outing in the wild.

Although you may vary a few items on the list to suit different types of trips, the Ten Essentials provide you with the basic tools to survive an unexpected emergency and make many difficulties more tolerable.

If you take a side trip for a day hike away from your basecamp however, your Ten Essentials will do you very little good if they are sitting in your tent while you are several miles away. Packing them in a small fanny-pack or stuff sack will make it easy to keep them with you.

MAP
Preferably a route map, trail guide and/or a topographic map of the smallest possible scale with the intended route marked, as well as camp sites, problem areas, and access and egress routes.

COMPASS
Any good-quality, liquid-filled compass is sufficient if you know how to use it. When you use your compass, **TRUST IT,** even if your "instinct," "gut feeling," or "inner sense of direction" contradicts it. You will err far more frequently than your compass will.

FLASHLIGHT
A small, lightweight flashlight is sufficient, but don't forget fresh batteries. A flashlight is obviously useful at night, but it is also a good signaling tool.

EMERGENCY FOOD & WATER
Emergency food need not be elaborate or even delectable, but it should be relatively non-perishable food (not just candy) capable of providing energy and a fed, if not full, feeling. Jerky, dried fruit, and granola

bars are possibilities. Water must be purified and well sealed to avoid leaks. Even a pint can help a lot.

SUPPLEMENTAL CLOTHING & SHELTER

Wool hat, gloves, and socks are useful extras. Adding lightweight long underwear gives you the flexibility to tolerate a much greater temperature range. A tube tent or space blanket will work well for shelter. Include some parachute cord for rigging.

SUNGLASSES, SUNSCREEN AND/OR INSECT REPELLENT

Each of these can prevent debilitating problems. Glasses protect eyes from irritation, prevent headaches, and improve visibility. Use sunscreen rated at least 15. Sunburn can be painful, extremely taxing on energy and may occur rapidly and severely even when not expected. Insect repellent should have a DEET content of at least 30 percent to repel the worst of the biting bugs.

KNIFE

The most useful of tools. Size is less important than versatility. The Swiss-Army type is ideal.

MATCHES

Both the wooden type and the waterproof ones should be in a watertight case. A useful addition is a disposable cigarette lighter for everyday use. Keep the matches as a back-up.

FIRESTARTER

Not an insult to woodsmanship, a firestarter is vital for starting a fire quickly when you are cold, wet, and not concerned with demonstrating skill. Pastes, gels, or simply a candle stub work fine. A bit of "birch" bark or other dry tinder in a waterproof bag is also a good idea.

FIRST AID KIT

Keep it simple but include small dressings, aspirin, a cortisone or other anti-itch cream, and blister care supplies like moleskin or Spenco Second-Skin. Remember to carry any personal medications that may be needed.

CAMPSITE SELECTION

In spite of your best efforts, the chances that you'll find a campsite that meets all of the criteria for an optimum place to camp in the wild are somewhere between slim and none.

Ideally, you'd like a spot that's level, smooth and dry, near a good water source and a plentiful firewood supply, open to fresh air in summer, sheltered from the winds in winter, pristine, unspoiled, and blessed with a spectacular view. So would everybody else out there! You'll have to settle for something less than ideal. Just remember to look for the most important features that will ensure your physical safety and basic comfort.

The most important features of an acceptable campsite include flat and relatively smooth ground and a place that will be dry to the extent that you won't be washed away by an overnight flash flood or a rising tide. Second in importance is placement with respect to the wind—exposed to keep cool and free from bugs or sheltered from an impending storm.

In the vast majority of backcountry areas, you'll find places where others have camped before you. Since there are simply too many people out there for each of us too have an unused site, the best choice is to find a "used" campsite that is well placed and not too badly damaged. Reusing an old site virtually guarantees that the spot will be significantly damaged, perhaps for many years to come, but it limits the damage to just on place. It's a tough choice, but in all but the most remote wilderness areas, it's far better to put up with not being first at the spot than to further extend human damage.

If you're far enough off the beaten track that there's no previously-used site, find a new site where damage will be minimized. Sand, gravel, rock, or rocky soil are most resistant to long-term damage from camping. Forest duff with no vegetation is an acceptable alternative.

Try not to camp on vegetation. The pressure of a person sleeping for even one night may compress the moisture-holding layers of soil enough to cause severe

The Camper's Pocket Handbook

restriction of plant growth for a long time. Alpine meadows and tundra are particularly vulnerable to this type of damage and are very slow to heal.

CAMP SANITATION

Sloppy campsites are not only ugly and smell bad, they may pollute water and threaten the health of other campers and wildlife. It's easy to maintain a clean pleasant camp. Here's how.

LATRINES

Small groups staying in one place for one night probably do not need an established latrine. Each person should use the "cat-hole" method:

1. Move at least 200 feet from any water source, trails, or campsites.
2. Move a small rock or log and dig a hole 4"–6" deep in the bare spot beneath it.
3. After use, burn toilet paper if you can do so safely (it speeds decomposition), refill the hole, and replace the rock or log on top of it.
4. Sanitary napkins and tampons must be burned or packed out.

Larger groups or established camps need a group site consisting of a hole about one foot wide and no more than eighteen inches deep, placed at least 200 feet from any water source, trail, or campsite. Diapers, sanitary napkins, and tampons must be burned or packed out.

FISH REMAINS

Clean fish well away from the campsite and downwind. Bury fish remains. A variety of animals may be attracted to the odor of your fish. None of them will be welcome in your campsite.

TRASH

All trash must be packed out if it cannot be **COMPLETELY** burned. Many food packages contain some non-burnable foil but they can be greatly reduced in weight and odor by burning. It's OK to burn them to make it easier to pack out. Just don't forget to gather the foil remains the next morning! And that includes trash that some slob left before you got there.

Small amounts of leftover food may be buried in a latrine.

DISH WASHING

Dishes must be washed daily in hot water and rinsed completely. If the water is hot, soap is not really needed. If you must use it though, use only a natural, biodegradable type and use very little. If no pot scrubber is handy, a bit of sand or fine gravel is a good substitute.

Wash water may be discarded in thick vegetation.

Don't let any soap, even the biodegradable kind, get into water sources.

BATHING

A daily bath is delightfully refreshing and good for you. Although we all like to be a part of nature, there's no reason nature has to cling to you for days on end to complete the experience. Forget the macho image of the crusty mountain man. Getting clean feels great at the end of a day! Don't pass up the opportunity!

The best way to bathe in the wilds is to first take a dip to get wet, then get out of the water and move a short distance away to soap up. Here again, soap is not always necessary. A good scrubbing does wonders without it. If you use soap, use just a little on the "critical" areas only. Pour water over yourself to rinse. Don't swim off the suds or let any soap get into a water source! A final swim after rinsing is the best part.

TOOTHPASTE

When you brush your teeth (don't forget to use purified water), spit the toothpaste on the ground and pour leftover water on it to disperse the toothpaste residue. Do not let toothpaste get into any water source.

TENT PLACEMENT & SET-UP

In any campsite, the tent should be placed well away from the food preparation and eating areas, on the flattest possible portion of the campsite, and with the door facing downwind. If snow is blowing, the door should be at a right angle to the wind to void a snow-drift building in front of the door.

Put a waterproof groundsheet inside the tent, not under it. Most holes in tent floors come from the inside, and body pressure frequently causes water to come up through the floor in spite of the best water-proof fabrics and seam sealing techniques. Placing the groundsheet inside solves both problems. If your groundsheet is somewhat larger than the floor area of the tent, as it should be, let the sides of the ground sheet curl up along the side of the tent. If any water does get in, it won't flow over the edge of the ground-sheet and get to you.

STORM-RIGGING YOUR TENT

With the exception of the most expensive mountain tents, very few tents are stable enough to withstand a substantial storm without some additional reinforce-ment. Anytime a storm is brewing, it is safest to expect the worst and start "battening down the hatch-es" early. If you haven't modified your tent for storm-rigging (an evening project at home with the sewing machine), you can still make some improvements to help your tent withstand a storm.

Start by adding at least two additional ropes to each end of the tent. Tie the ropes to the frame of the

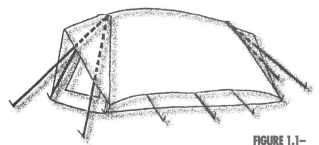

FIGURE 1.1–
Storm Rigging Your Tent

Add two extra lines to the tent frame front and rear.

Add at least one extra line to the fly on each side.

tent, not to D rings or tie loops on the tent fabric that may tear out in a gusty wind. Incorporating a loop of shock cord in the ropes helps to absorb the hard buffeting of the wind.

Add at least one extra rope along each side extending from the edge of the rainfly. Here you may have to make do with tying to a ring or tie loop on the fabric.

In a pinch, you can create a makeshift tie point on a tent fly or tarp. Place a small rock under the fabric a few inches from the edge. Pull the fabric down over the rock and tie around the base of it. Unfortunately, this method is wickedly abrasive on the fabric and will probably cause some damage. But, in a big storm, it may help keep you in your campsite.

EMERGENCY SHELTERS

TARPS & TARP RIGGING

An 8' x 10' or 10' x 10' lightweight coated nylon tarp is an excellent emergency shelter. But as most of us carry tents into the outback, and tents have a pretty fair record of holding together, the tarp is most frequently used to make camp more comfortable. We don't care how good your raingear is or how weatherproof your tent, the simple fact is that cooking in a hard rain is dog work. And stuffing the occupants of three two-person tents into one tent for a bull session in the rain just doesn't cut it. That is when the tarp is worth its weight.

The best way to pitch a tarp is over a ridgeline, to establish a "pitched roof." If you plan to set the tarp up over the entry of your tent, angle the ridgeline up so water running off the tarp winds up on the ground and not on the tent.

It's possible to build a small fire under a tarp. The angled ridgeline will serve as a chimney if the wind isn't howling, and you'll be able to cook, chat, and relax in a (relatively) dry and smokeless environment.

If you have two tarps, overlap the ridgelines by two to three feet and guy each tarp separately. Sure, it takes a few minutes to do this, but, when the rain keeps on coming, the small effort is worth it. There are few things in life that can make you feel as smug as being dry and well-fed in the outback when the rain is hammering down!

NOTE THIS: *If you keep your tarp in its very own stuff bag and keep that stuff bag readily accessible, it makes a great shelter for a trailside lunch, too. Rig it from trees, rig it from ski poles, rig it from paddles, lash off one end of it to an overturned canoe—anything to keep you dry while you're chowing down. Even if you're already damp around the edges, the psychological benefits of a dry and wind-free lunch are very nearly incalculable.*

TUBE TENTS

Tube tents are cylinders of plastic sheeting, and are good emergency shelters. Set-up is by means of a single rope tied to two trees and run down the middle of the tube tent about 3 feet above the ground. The shape of the tent is held by the equipment and people inside.

NATURAL SHELTERS

While usually far from comfortable, a natural shelter may be an important key to your survival.

CAVES & OVERHANGS

In many areas you can find shallow rock caves or overhangs along rocky gullies, canyons, and outcroppings. Such caves may have to be cleared of rocks and debris, but the material may be piled up for wind protection on the open side.

If an electrical storm is brewing, be very cautious of shallow caves in exposed areas. If the cave is not deeper than it is tall, ground currents from a nearby lightning strike may go through the cave rather than going around or skipping over the opening.

If warmth is needed, it's most effective to sleep between the fire and the rock wall. This also lets you put the fire near the cave opening for best ventilation.

FALLEN TREES

In forested areas there may be large fallen trees that can be made to serve as a shelter. The best ones are at least 2 feet in diameter and have some room under them or beside them to sit and be fairly sheltered.

A roof may be built with branches or large bark slabs in a lean-to fashion. Such a roof will leak some rain but is a worthwhile effort to hold in heat. Be very cautious with fires!

If there are large evergreen trees that have branches hanging to the ground, you can often find a cozy shelter next to the trunk of the tree under the overhanging

The Camper's Pocket Handbook

branches. Some branches may have to be cleared away from the open area underneath, but they can be used to reinforce the "walls" of the shelter.

INSECT PESTS

In the perpetual war against biting insects, the most effective weapons are well-sealed, light-colored clothing, insect repellents with at least 30 percent DEET *(n, n-diethyl-metoluamide),* and a positive mental attitude. Don't let the little buggers get you down!

Dark colors such as navy blue, beloved of outdoor people (hey, it doesn't show the dirt!), tend to attract bugs while lighter, more neutral colors do not. Bright colors like yellow seem to have a slight repelling effect. Your choice. Be ecologically invisible and get bitten, or be gaudy and bug-free.

All clothing should be tightly woven and openings around neck, sleeves, and cuffs should be sewn shut or sealed with Velcro.

Repellents with high DEET concentration may irritate sensitive skin and cause allergic reactions and will dissolve some plastics like glasses frames and watch bands and some synthetic fabrics such as polypropylene underwear. Avoid getting the stuff on your lips, too. It tastes terrible! And there's evidence that DEET concentrations much above 30 percent don't add to a repellent's effectiveness.

To avoid bugs around your face and head, soak a

cotton bandana with repellent, tie it around your neck, and wear a headnet. Concentrate repellent near cuffs of clothing where bugs may try to burrow in, as well as on and around your ears, a favorite target area of black flies.

In the final analysis however, the bugs are going to be there, and some are going to bite you. Accept them as a mildly irritating drawback that comes with something you love, and learn to make the best of it.

It can't be all coincidence that on any given wilderness trip, those who seem most worried and concerned about the bugs always get bitten the most. The person who couldn't seem to care less and just slops on repellent and goes on about enjoying the outback remains relatively unscathed.

CAMP BEARS

Noted outdoorsman Cliff Jacobson* advises that the old and well known methods of hiding food from bears does not work when you are in areas where bears are accustomed to campers such as in and around many major parks. In such places, the techniques of hiding food in trees are as well-known to the bears as to campers, and the bears can be very creative in finding ways to get to it.

---

* Consult Cliff Jacobson's *Camping's Top Secrets, second edition* (Globe Pequot Press, P.O. Box 833, Old Saybrook, CT 06475–0833) for a complete depiction of bear-proofing your packs. The book is available at your favorite outdoor outfitter.

The Camper's Pocket Handbook

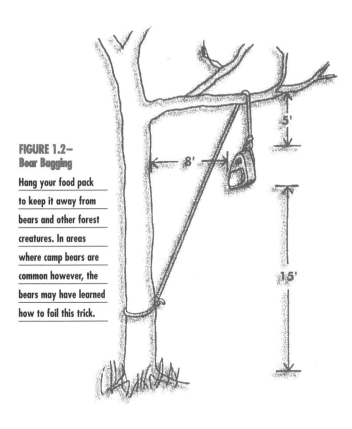

**FIGURE 1.2–
Bear Bagging**

Hang your food pack
to keep it away from
bears and other forest
creatures. In areas
where camp bears are
common however, the
bears may have learned
how to foil this trick.

5'

8'

15'

Cliff suggests placing food packs where the bears are not in the habit of looking and being certain to eliminate any escape of odors from the food that would tip the bear off to where the food is hidden.

Seal all food in double plastic bags to eliminate odors. Place the food packs or bags on the ground well outside the camp area. Place packs at least 50 feet apart and down low where they will look like a rock or a bush to a bear (who is naturally near-sighted) and will also avoid spreading odors in the wind.

The tried and true method of hanging your food pack, usually known as "Bear Bagging," also works well if you follow the rules. Find a tall tree with an overhanging branch or run a line between two trees to give you a place from which you can hang the food pack at least 15 feet off the ground and 8 feet away from the trunk of each tree. If it is at least 5 feet down from the limb's well, the bear cannot climb out on the limb and reach it.

LiTTLE ANiMAL PESTS

Everybody worries about bears, and it probably makes good sense to show some concern about anything that's two to three times bigger than you, faster than you, and capable of learning from experience. But it is a good bet that it won't be bears that mess up your pack and eat everything in sight. It'll be little critters like squirrels, chipmunks, and raccoons.

We assume that you have the sense that God fave a goose, which is to say, you're not going to bring four Hershey bars with almonds (is there any other kind??) into your tent so Big Bad Bruin can nibble on whatever of you is close to the candy. Fine. This keeps bruin out of your tent and also little critters that simply gnaw through the tent wall to get at your food.

Hanging a pack will help keep the little guys at bay, but it won't be infallible, as anybody who's ever tried to keep squirrels out of a bird feeder will tell you. And Cliff's trick of keeping your food in double plastic bags will help, as will keeping your food in tins or plastic containers with close fitting tops. The bad news is that nothing is foolproof. The good news is that the little critters are cute and with the exception of 'coon, prefer to forage in the daytime. Give up, watch, and enjoy.

If all else fails, try a small offering of peanuts left well outside the perimeter of camp, and stand guard with a camera.

BuiLDiNG YOUR CAMPFiRE

Although a small camp stove should be used for most cooking, there are times when a campfire might be desired, though not always wise, and there are times when one might be desperately needed. A roaring campfire may be a life-saving necessity to treat a victim of hypothermia, and in areas where sufficient firewood is available, there is no better way to end a day in the wild than by sitting around a small campfire watching the stars come out. Check with local burn rules and always use a firepan.

The key to building a fire at any time and under any conditions is to take plenty of time to prepare the site and gather all your materials before you strike the first match.

PREPARE SITE

First find a place that's level, sheltered from the wind, and on a surface that will be fairly resistant to damage. This damage concern is more than just the possible wildfire hazard that is always so important. Your concern must also be directed to minimizing the scarring of earth and rock to protect the natural beauty of the area.

Admittedly a firepan is the best device to minimize impact; however, long distance hikers might not have this luxury. If you can, find a surface of sand or gravel which can be easily stirred around afterward to disperse the ashes and ease the fire scar. Second choices would include removal of a section of sod or scraping away forest duff to expose bare clay or mineral soil. In those cases, once the fire is dead out, the sod can be replaced or the forest litter scattered about to return the spot to muck like its natural condition.

Avoid forest duff, peat, and humus soil as a fire surface. On those surfaces, the damage caused by a controlled camp fire is substantial and long-lasting. Even worse, though, is that the chances of uncontrolled fire erupting out of long-smouldering ashes are considerable. Fire travels underground in these soils. Even a thorough soaking of the firepit may not extinguish all the fire.

If necessary, a base layer of sand or gravel at least 3 inches thick may be laid on top of a poorer surface, and a small fire may be built on that base. This requires a great deal of caution to be sure the fire does not "migrate" off the base, and after the fire is dead out, the base material must be returned to where it was found.

In all cases, clear away all burnable material in a wide circle around the fire site, preferably at least 10 feet in diameter.

SELECT WOOD

Softwoods (the evergreens) make good kindling and tinder because they flare quickly. Softwoods burn up pretty fast however, and they create a bit of smoke as well. You'll also find the softwoods prone to popping and throwing sparks depending on the moisture content in the wood.

Hardwoods have flat leaves rather than needles or scales. Hardwoods burn longer and steadier than softwoods and make much better coals for cooking.

Even after days of soaking rain, dry wood can be found inside dead limbs and trees that have not been lying on the ground soaking up moisture and rotting. Check the margins of wooded areas for dead limbs or trees that are up off the ground and have been exposed to sunlight.

Wet logs, even floating ones, will nearly always have a dry center from which burnable wood can be split. Saw the limb or tree into 1-2 foot sections and split the dry center wood into kindling. Don't—please!—flail at the wood with an axe or hatchet to split it! Drive the axe head through the wood with a stout 2-foot long club. It saves toes, fingers, and the edge of the tool as well.

GATHER MATERIALS & LAY FOUNDATION

Gather a large handful of twigs, shavings, or splits in sizes from the thickness of a wooden match (or smaller) to no larger than a lead pencil. A few strips of birch bark (from dead trees or sticks only) or dry tinder like cattail fluff, shredded dead grass, or shredded twigs is also a good idea.

Find or split a large armful of kindling ranging from the size of a lead pencil to the thickness of your finger.

Gather at least twice as much wood as you think you will need, in sizes from the size of your finger to the size of your wrist. Larger wood is seldom useful for a campfire.

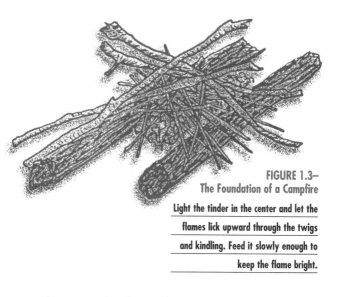

FIGURE 1.3–
The Foundation of a Campfire

Light the tinder in the center and let the
flames lick upward through the twigs
and kindling. Feed it slowly enough to
keep the flame bright.

Choose two kindling sticks that are about the thickness of your finger and lay them parallel on the fire site about 3" apart. Lay the handful of twigs with the bark or dry tinder under them at a right angle across the two sticks, and crush them together in a fairly tight wad. The kindling sticks should hold the twigs up just enough to get a match or lighter under them.

Lay 3 or 4 small pieces of kindling on top of the wad of twigs.

LIGHT THE FIRE

Shield the fire from wind and use a wooden match, lighter, or candle to hold a flame under the twigs and allow the flame to lick far up into the wad of timber.

Gently add small pieces of kindling as the flames begin to reach through the top of the wad of tinder. Avoid smothering by leaving a space between the sticks that is at least 1/2 the thickness of the stick.

MAINTAIN THE FIRE

Gradually add larger sticks as the fire grows, remembering to allow space between the sticks.

Do not make the fire larger than necessary. Feed it steadily rather than building a raging inferno and letting it die to coals before building it up again.

MAKE COALS FOR COOKING

Use sound hardwood sticks split to a uniform thickness of about 1" to ½".

Stack them over a smaller fire in a criss-cross fashion about 1 foot high. Allow them to burn down to a pile of coals with no visible flame.

PUT THE FIRE OUT

Allow the fire to burn itself out as much as possible.

Remove any wood pieces not completely burned and pour water over them until they're cool enough to touch.

Stir the coals deeply to loosen all the compacted coals and hot dirt.

Sprinkle water over the fire while continuing to stir the ashes. Continue soaking until all smoke and steam is gone and the entire fire site is cool to touch.

Remove any particles of unburned trash and pack them out.

WINTER CAMPING

Camping in winter requires greater attention to detail and a slower, more methodical approach too routine tasks. Take extra care to avoid unnecessary exposure to the elements and avoid any nonessential activities that may use up your valuable energy.

To sleep warmer, try eating one hour before going to bed. Immediately after eating, your body uses a great deal of energy for digestion. An hour or so later, though, most all energy will be available for warmth.

A make-shift vapor-barrier liner can be very effective if your feet are cold. Simply put a plastic bag over your foot and under your socks. Moisture and warmth will be held in, and your socks will stay drier and will insulate better.

Pay particular attention to keeping your head warm. Since heat always rises, your head and neck act like a radiator and can be responsible for nearly 50% of the heat loss from your body. Here's a hint.

A lightweight woolen stocking cap or a Navy-style watch cap worn in your sleeping bag can keep you wonderfully cozy on a damp, chilly night.

Insulate your water bottles by slipping them inside wool socks. If you store the bottle upside down, ice will not plug the bottle neck.

Avoiding Moisture Build-up

When you are camping in the cold be sure that you make every effort to keep moisture, whether from the outside or the inside (sweat), from getting into your clothing or any insulating layers. It is true to some extent that wool and some synthetic insulations are warm when wet, but no one ever said that they meant comfortably warm. At best, wet insulation will keep you only survivably warm and intensely miserable.

Take care to brush all snow off your clothing before you get into the tent. If you don't, the snow will melt, making your clothing damp and increasing the overall moisture build-up in the tent.

Keep the tent well-ventilated to disperse any accumulating moisture. It's a curious fact that a slight breeze through the tent can end up keeping you warmer. Don't put damp clothing in a sleeping bag either by wearing it or trying to dry it. The moisture will move to the insulation of the sleeping bag and stay there, reducing the warmth of the bag.

Don't cover your mouth and nose in the sleeping

The Camper's Pocket Handbook

bag. The moisture from your breath will be trapped in the bag. A scarf or balaclava may be worn to keep your face warm.

Wear layered clothes that can easily be adjusted to avoid overheating and can be ventilated to release trapped moisture.

When you're exercising in the cold, the key to staying warm is to open your clothing to ventilate accumulating moisture, or remove clothing layers **BEFORE** the inner layers of clothing get damp. At times however, such as when the wind is very strong and the wind-chill is substantial, it may not be wise to remove much clothing for ventilation, because you may chill very quickly or even risk frostbite. In that situation, the best alternative is to slow your pace down to the point that you're just active enough to stay warm but not sweating enough to let moisture accumulate in your clothing.

WINTER CAMPSITE SELECTION

The shortened daylight of winter calls for early camp setup to allow time to get settled before dark. Since every camp chore takes much longer in the winter, allow yourself at least one hour before sunset to make camp. In the morning, plan on at least two hours to pack and break camp.

Snow creates new campsites that are not available in warmer weather and greatly reduces the potential damage to the ground and plant life. Snow may also hide hazards such as crevasses and small streams, however.

If snow is loose, stamp around the campsite with your skis or snowshoes on to compact the snow before you set up your tent. If the snow is too dry to pack down, scrape it down to a firm surface.

To avoid problems with drifting snow, don't place the tent door downwind. The door should be placed at an angle or perpendicular to the wind. Excavating the tent somewhat into deep snow will also reduce drifting.

Tent pegs may be anchored in snow by packing a wet snowball around the tent peg and burying it in the snow to freeze. A hole may also be chopped into frozen ground and water poured in with the stake to freeze it into place.

EMERGENCY SNOW SHELTER

If you are forced to make camp in the snow without a tent, you must construct a shelter of some sort. The easiest and fastest snow shelter is a snow trench.

Dig a trench in the snow 3' to 4' deep, about 3' wide and long enough to lie down in.

Place several wood poles, skis, ski poles, or other items across the trench and cover with a plastic sheet or tarp.

Anchor and cover the roof with a thin layer of snow for insulation.

WALKING TECHNIQUES

Virtually every trip to the backcountry includes some walking, and frequently you will be walking for extended distances while carrying a heavy load. While walking in civilization presents few problems, safe and efficient walking in the wild requires some thought and planning.

Back around the turn of the century, Europe and North America had their first "bicycle boom." As the middle and upper classes had just spent the better part of the century before escaping physical labor as fast as they could, a lot of the new bicyclists didn't know much about their bodies worked under physical stress. A French bicycle aficionado—a working-class gent named Paul de Vivie who wrote widely and well under the pen name of Velocio—formulated some rules of travel that made sense then and make sense today, whether your conveyance is a mountain bike, a canoe, skis, snowshoes, or Shank's mare. And here they are:

1. Eat *before* you're hungry.
2. Drink *before* you're thirsty.
3. Peel off *before* you're sweaty.
4. Put on *before* you're chilly.
5. Rest *before* you're tired.
6. Avoid tobacco and alcohol while on tour.
7. Don't just tour to prove you can do it.

If you made old Velocio's rules a part of your thinking, John Goll and Harry Roberts wouldn't have much to write about. Well—we could expand on the rules.

STRETCHING

Before you walk or carry a pack for any distance, some brief stretching and warmup will go a long way to prevent injuries. Gently stretch your leg muscles by slowly and smoothly extending or stretching the muscle to the point of resistance (not pain) and holding there for 20 to 30 seconds. Remember to include your upper body and back in the "limbering up" process.

SETTING THE PACE

The speed of walking should be governed by your exertion, not time or distance goals. Changing your pace to keep exertion constant will produce the most travel for the least energy spent. Go slowly enough that you're comfortable breathing with your mouth closed.

In rugged areas, it may help to count the number of breaths per step to help watch and control your pace. On the flats, 3 to 4 steps per breath may work well, while on hills 1 or 2 steps per breath may be better. On steep climbs, 3 or 4 breaths per step is not unusual. Slow your pace before fatigue forces you to.

You can save a surprising amount of energy by not stepping up onto anything that you can step over. A high step takes much more energy than a longer one.

Whenever possible, avoid routes that go directly up or downhill. Use an angle or zig-zagging switchback pattern to ease the steepness of the slope.

WALKING SAFELY

You can avoid falls by being cautious of placing your weight on fallen trees or potentially unstable rocks. Moisture, ice, wet leaves and moss make many surfaces surprisingly slippery. A handful of sand thrown on such slippery surfaces may help traction.

When traveling downhill, keep your knees bent and your center of gravity low and back. Use a switchback pattern rather than walking straight down the fall line if possible. Side-stepping may be the safest choice for steep slopes.

RESTING

Rests should be frequent and don't need to be too long. With proper pacing, brief 5-minute pauses about once an hour will be sufficient to keep traveling for some time. But it's nice to take a little more time when you can. Don't forget why you came to the backcountry in the first place! If all you do is cover distance while staring at the trail, you'll miss the experience of getting to know the country and letting yourself become part of it.

Drink some water at every stop. When you can, remove your pack and elevate your feet for awhile. If possible, remove your boots and socks to allow your feet to dry and stimulate circulation. Briefly washing your feet in cool water can be very refreshing, but take care not to soak them too long which may soften the skin and promote blisters.

COURTESY WITH PACK ANIMALS & HORSES

Pack animals and horses may be somewhat unpredictable and hard to control when they meet strangers on the trail. They should be allowed the right-of-way. When meeting them, stand several feet off to one side and remain quiet and still as they pass. To a horse, a person with a large pack may look very different from the people he is used to seeing. Don't speak unless the rider speaks, and do not make any gestures towards the animal.

PRESERVING TRAILS

To reduce trail erosion and deterioration, don't stray off established trails. Stay in the main travel groove waling single-file. Even a very few persons walking the edges of a trail will quickly magnify damage to plant growth and greatly increase erosion damage.

Don't wear lug-soled boots unless you really need them for safe traction. The deep lugs dig soil out of trails and cut badly into tender plants and roots.

CROSSING STREAMS

First, stop and decide whether you really must cross the stream right there. Stream crossings are never without some risk. There may be an easier spot up-stream or downstream. A wide and shallow area is far better than a narrow and deep one.

If at all possible, streams that are very fast, cold, or more than knee-deep should not be waded. Moving water is surprisingly powerful and dangerous.

When you cross a stream, release the waist belt of your pack and loosen the straps so the pack can be thrown off quickly in the event of a fall.

Take your socks off, but wear your boots when wading to protect your feet. Taking your socks off before you wade and putting them back on afterward will keep your feet warmer than soaking your socks underwater.

A stout pole may be used as a "third leg" for additional support. Face upstream with the pole in front and side-step across.

A fixed rope, tied across the stream as a handhold may be helpful. Stay on the downstream side of the rope.

NEVER tie a rope to a person crossing a stream. If the person falls, as the rope holds them fast, the current will push them to the bottom.

CROSSING ICE

As with stream crossings, stop and think about it. Crossing ice, especially in unfamiliar territory can be very risky. Be especially cautious if the ice is over or near a stream or river. Moving water often keeps ice from freezing thick enough to walk on.

To safely support one person, ice must be at least 2 inches thick. To support several people spread out in a line, ice must be 3 inches thick.

If your group must cross ice, keep people at least 20 feet apart, and each one should carry a long pole. The pole may be used to test the ice ahead and, in the event of a fall, the pole may bridge across the hole to keep the person from falling all the way under. A pole may also be used to reach someone who has fallen through the ice.

UNPLANNED SNOW TRAVEL

Avoid walking across snow if you aren't equipped with skis or snowshoes. Trying to do so will be inconvenient, difficult, and potentially dangerous.

Spring snow in the process of melting is wet and sloppy, with the possibility of dangerous hollows beneath it that may be quite deep. Try to avoid walking near trees or rocks that project up through the snow. Especially when it's sunny, they may conduct enough warmth downward to melt a large hollow area around the base covered with a roof of snow too thin to support your weight. Small springs beneath the snow may also cause hollows with no indication on the surface.

If you must travel over deep snow, it's safest in the

morning before the warmth of the sun softens the snow. Makeshift snowshoes may be made by tying broad evergreen boughs to your feet. While neither efficient nor comfortable, they will help keep you from sinking in the snow as much and will save a good deal of energy.

BASIC KNOTS

Virtually all tying, rigging, and securing of loads with rope can be done with a few basic knots.

TWO HALF-HITCHES

Two half-hitches are often used as a starting tie for a rope that will secure a load. Although very strong, two half-hitches can be pulled tight enough to make them difficult to untie unless a quick-release loop is used.

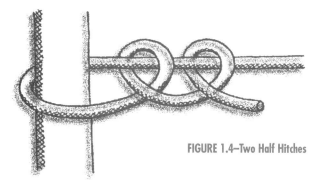

FIGURE 1.4–Two Half Hitches

POWER CINCH

Often called a Trucker's Hitch, Cliff Jacobson dubbed this knot the Power Cinch to accurately describe its basic function, that of powerfully tightening a load while remaining very easy to untie.

The first step is to place a Quick-Release Knot in the rope that is holding the load.

Then pass the rope around the securing point and back through the Quick-Release Knot.

Pulling back on the loose end of the rope will tighten the rope with the effect of a pulley system with a 2:1 mechanical advantage.

Finally secure the loose end against the loop with a Quick-Release Knot or Two Half-Hitches.

SHEET BEND

The Sheet Bend will tie any two ropes together, even ones that are different sizes, and will always be easy to untie.

The free ends of both ropes should be on the same side of the knot for maximum strength.

BOWLINE

The Bowline is by far the best knot to use for putting a loop at the end of a rope. It is absolutely secure and has for years been a basic knot for climbing purposes.

The free end should come out on the inside of the loop to ensure the strongest knot.

QUICK-RELEASE KNOT

The Quick-Release Knot is fast and convenient and, because it can be untied with one quick pull of the loose end, it has thousands of uses. It is frequently used to secure other knots such as the Power Cinch *(below)* or as a quick means of tying a tarp rigging line or any securing job that needs to be quickly and easily untied.

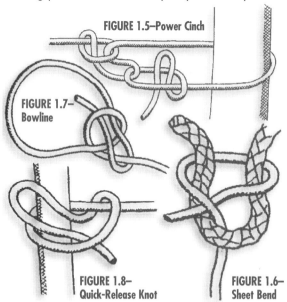

FIGURE 1.5–Power Cinch

FIGURE 1.7– Bowline

FIGURE 1.8– Quick-Release Knot

FIGURE 1.6– Sheet Bend

2 ROUTE FINDING

Do You Know the Way to…?

it should be reasonably obvious that you need to know where you are and where you're going at all times. The basic tools for route finding include a map, a compass, a watch, and a working knowledge of how to use them. And thoughtful observation, while difficult to quantify, won't hurt you. Electronic Global Positioning System (GPS) devices are entertaining and sometimes useful tools, but they are no substitute for a map and compass.

MAP BASICS

Topographic maps are usually preferred for wilderness travel. In well-traveled areas, commercial route or trail maps may be sufficient if you don't stray far off the beaten path where they may show little, if any, detail of the terrain.

All maps use a variety of symbols to illustrate features and provide information about; the area. Before using any map, and especially when trying to figure out navigation problems, refer to the key to be sure you are interpreting the map symbols correctly. Maps are rarely significantly wrong. Many of the errors that occur in map reading are the result o misinterpreting the symbols and codes on the map.

Other important information on topographic maps include the map scale, contour lines, true north, and magnetic declination.

MAP SCALE

The scale of a map is the proportion of distance on the map to distance on the ground. The scale may be shown by a linechart, a ratio, or both. A ratio like "1:24,000" for example, means that any one unit of measure on the map equals the larger number of units of the same measure on the ground. (1 inch on the map equals 24,000 inches on the ground.)

COMMON U.S. & CANADIAN TOPOGRAPHIC MAP SCALES

1:24,000	(7.5 minute quadrangle) 1 inch + about 2,000 feet; 2 $^1/_4$ inches = about one mile
1:50,000	1 $^1/_4$ inches = 1 mile

1:62,500   (15 minute quadrangle) 1 inch = 1 mile

....

1:250,000   1 inch = 4 miles

....

CONTOUR LINES AND INTERVAL

The light brown lines that distinguish a topographic map are contour lines. Contour lines connect points of equal elevation and create a three-dimensional picture of the land.

On some maps, every fifth contour line is darker and has the elevation of that line above sea level printed along it.

The contour interval, indicated at the bottom of the map, is the elevation difference between the contour lines. Contour intervals may be in meters on Canadian maps. (1 meter = about 3.3 feet.)

When looking at a topographic map, you can form a mental picture of the "lay of the land" by remembering that the closer that contour lines are together, the steeper the slope and that well-spaced lines indicate gently sloping or flat terrain.

You can also tell which direction a stream or river flows by looking at the contour lines as they cross it. The lines will virtually always make a "V" shape as it crosses the water. The "V" will be pointing upstream.

TRUE NORTH

On a topographic map, true north is indicated by the right and left borders which correspond to lines of longitude. The small hash marks along the top and bottom borders of the map also indicate lines of longitude. You can easily indicate true north at the center of your map by drawing a line from the longitude marker at the top to the identically-labeled marker at the bottom.

If the area of the map is relatively far north, the right and left borders may not be parallel but may be closer together at the top. This is because the lines of longitude come together at the north pole.

For accurate compass work, be sure that compass readings from the map are taken using only the reference lines of longitude and not other lines or grids that may be on the map. The only exceptions to this is if you have corrected your map for declination by drawing adjusted north-south lines as described below.

Many topographic maps have a grid of horizontal and vertical lines that are there for certain surveying uses only. Do not use any of the lines in that grid for your navigation purposes!

MAGNETIC NORTH AND DECLINATION

The north magnetic pole is on Bathurst Island in Canada's Northwest Territories, about 1200 miles away from the true north pole (about 100 degrees west longitude and 76 degrees north latitude). Since a compass always points toward magnetic north, in most places there is a difference (declination) between magnetic north and true north.

The agonic line is an imaginary line along which magnetic north is virtually the same as true north. The agonic line runs roughly southeast from Bathurst Island through Churchill, Manitoba, Thunder Bay, Ontario, Indiana, and Florida.

In the eastern U.S. and Canada (east of the agonic line), magnetic north is several degrees west of true north (west declination). In the western U.S. and Canada (west of the agonic line), magnetic north is several degrees east of true north (east declination).

DECLINATION DIAGRAM

The declination for the center of the map is shown in the border of the map, usually with a small diagram, and the number of degrees that magnetic north is east or west of true north.

The number of degrees shown should be used for all calculations. The pictured angle of declination on the diagram is only a rough illustration and is not accurate for navigating.

CORRECTING FOR DECLINATION

In all compass work that compares the bearings on a map with bearings in the field, a correction for declination must be made. Failing to account for even small declinations can result in substantial errors over distance.

There are several ways to correct for declination. Be sure to use some method of correcting for declination, but use only one method.

COMPASS ADJUSTMENT

If you happen to have a compass with a declination adjustment screw, you need only set it for the declination of the area you are traveling in and forget any other worries about declination correction.

Once your compass is set, you do not need, nor should you make, any other corrections to maps, bearings, or anything. Your course bearings can be transferred directly from map to field and from field to map.

The declination on the compass must be re-set, however, when moving to areas with different declination.

If you don't have a compass with a declination adjustment screw, you must either correct your maps OR you must correct each bearing that you take for declination before you act on it. Do not do both!

MAP CORRECTION

If your compass can't be set to adjust for declination, your map can be "adjusted" to do the same thing.

Check the degrees of declination indicated on the map and use a protractor to draw a series of parallel lines across the map at an angle from true north that is equal to the declination.

Compass bearings may then be taken from the map using the new lines showing magnetic declination rather than the lines of longitude indicating true north. Once this is done, you don't need to make any bearing corrections.

RECALCULATING BEARINGS

Recalculating each and every compass bearing for declination is the most time-consuming method to correct for declination, but it doesn't require a special compass or customized markings on the map.

To recalculate bearings, add or subtract the degrees of declination each time you take a bearing from the map and apply it to the field and vice-versa.

For bearings taken **FROM THE MAP** and applied **TO THE FIELD:**

1. If the declination is east, subtract the number of degrees from the bearing.
2. If the declination is west, add the number of degrees to the bearing.

A popular rhyme may be used to help remember this formula: "From map to field, **EAST** is **LEAST (SUBTRACT)** and **WEST** is **BEST (ADD).**"

For bearings taken **FROM THE FIELD** and applied **TO THE MAP,** the opposite must be done:

1. If the declination is east, add the number of degrees to the bearing.

The Camper's Pocket Handbook

2. If the declination is west, subtract the number of degrees from the bearing.

FINDING WHERE YOU ARE

The easiest way to find where you are is to keep track of your progress constantly on the map, comparing landmarks you can see with ones shown on the map.

In addition to easy landmarks like roads, lakes, and hilltops, you can also use your compass to find what direction ridges, valleys, or streams are pointing and find the corresponding features on the map. For example, assume that after correcting for declination, you can tell you're looking at a narrow valley that is pointing exactly northeast (45 degrees). A narrow valley shown on the map that also points that direction is likely the one you're looking at. Look at the country! That's why you're out there!

TRIANGULATION

Triangulation is the most precise method to pinpoint your location in the field with a map and compass. To perform triangulation you need to be able to see two landmarks that are shown on the map such as hilltops, mountain peaks, or islands.

Take compass bearings on both landmarks and correct them for declination.

Compute the reciprocal (opposite) of each bearing by adding 180 degrees if the bearing is less than

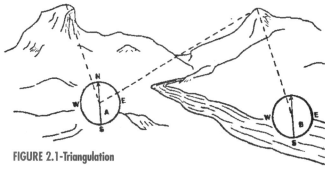

FIGURE 2.1-Triangulation

A. **Take bearings on two landmarks. Plot the reciprocal bearings on the map.**

Where the lines cross is your position.

B. **When you are at a long landmark, take a bearing on one other landmark.**

Plot the reciprocal bearing on the map.

Where the line crosses the long landmark is your position.

180, or subtracting 180 degrees if the bearing is greater than 180.

On the map, draw a line from the landmark sighted in the field along the reciprocal bearing for that landmark. Repeat the process for the other landmark. Your position will be where the two lines cross.

If you're near a river, road, power line, lakeshore, or other long feature that can be used as a baseline, and you can see just one other landmark that is shown on the map, a variation of the triangulation technique can be done.

Take a compass bearing on the landmark and correct it for declination.

Compute the reciprocal (opposite) of the bearing by adding 180 if the bearing is less than 180, or subtracting 180 if the bearing is greater than 180.

On the map, draw a line from the landmark along the reciprocal bearing.

Where the reciprocal bearing line crosses the baseline is your location.

TiMiNG PRoGRESS

To get and maintain a general idea of where you are, try to keep track of the amount of time you have traveled from your last known location.

Using your estimated speed and general direction of travel, you can get a general idea on the map of where you are. This is often helpful in locating landmarks that should be nearby so you can get an idea of which way to go to reach them.

As a very rough guide for planning, the chart of estimated travel speeds may be useful. Your actual rate of travel will certainly vary with your ability, fatigue and the number of distractions along the way.

Recheck your location at least every hour when traveling cross-country or when obvious landmarks are not available. By re-checking often you will find an arrow soon enough to back-track and correct it before you've wasted much time and energy.

ESTiMATED TRAVEL SPEEDS

WALKiNG

Level ground, moderate elevation, light load	4 mph
Over 6,000 feet elevation with some hills	3 mph
Cross-country without trails	1.5 mph
Steep climbing	1 mph

CANOEiNG

Lake travel with no wind	3-4 mph
Fast river with few portages	3-5 mph
Fast river with frequent portages	1-2 mph
Upstream with no wind,	less than 1 mph

SNOW TRAVEL

Cross-country skiing, no prepared trail	4 mph
Snowshoes in open country	2 mph

FIGURE 2.2

Going Where You Want To Go

The most accurate way to travel an exact course is to follow a specific bearing from point to point:

1. Find your exact location and your intended destination on the map.
2. Measure the bearing from your position directly to your destination. Correct the bearing for declination.
3. Set the direction of travel arrow on the compass to the corrected degree bearing for your route of travel.
4. Orient the compass so the needle aligns with north.
5. Keeping the compass needle on north, sign along the direction of travel arrow an pick out a nearby landmark or feature that is directly in line with the direction of travel arrow.
6. Keep your eyes on the landmark and proceed directly to it.
7. Sight another landmark or feature in the same manner and continue from one to another all the way to your destination.

While following an exact bearing from point to point is very accurate, it's time-consuming and is seldom needed unless you must find an exact spot in the midst of rather featureless or confusing terrain. (Picking out a specific spot on a map and trying to follow a course directly to it, however, is a great way to have a bit of fun, challenge yourself, and hone your skills at the same time.)

In most cases, a sufficiently accurate course can be followed by just setting the compass for the desired direction of travel and following it alone to your destination.

1. Find your exact location and your intended destination on the map.

2. Measure the bearing from your position directly to your destination. Correct the bearing for declination.

3. Set the direction of travel arrow on the compass to the corrected degree bearing for the route of travel.

4. Orient the compass on the needle aligns with north.

5. Keeping the compass needle on north, travel in the direction that the direction of travel arrow points.

This method is less accurate because it's possible, even likely, that you will drift to one side or the other of the direct line to your destination.

USING A BASELINE AND AIMING OFF

To travel away from, and later back to, a river, road, lakeshore, or other long landmark, the line of that landmark may be used as a baseline.

Compute the compass bearing to your destination and follow the bearing as usual.

When returning to the baseline, follow the reciprocal of the original bearing. Since some drifting to one side or the other is almost inevitable when traveling cross country, deliberately "aim off" to one side when returning. In this way you plan for your error so when you arrive back at the baseline, you will know which way to turn to get back to your starting point. It saves you from asking very embarrassing questions like, "Is the car up the road or down the road?" Of course, it's either dark or raining or both when you ask that question, right?

TROUBLESHOOTING NAVIGATION PROBLEMS

As soon as you notice that you're not sure where you are or how to get to your destination, take the time to stop and methodically re-check all potential trouble points until your questions are answered.

Recheck the map scale, the contour interval, all your declination corrections, and the possibility of changes by both man and nature since the map was made.

Find your last known position on the map and note

the time you were there and how much time has passed since then.

Note the general direction of travel when you left your last known position, estimate your rate of travel, and look for features on the map that match what you can see or that you may be able to find.

If you're unable to determine exactly where you are, but have a general idea, check the map for the nearest long landmark or baseline such as a road, river, large lake, or ridge.

Plot a course to it carefully. Plan exactly what you intend to find and what you will be able to see to indicate you are either finding or missing the landmark. Estimate the time that you will know that you have or have not found the landmark. Don't change plans midway. Carry them out completely before trying another plan.

If darkness or weather threatens, or if you're becoming tired, start preparations to camp overnight. Allow at least an hour of sunlight to make camp and prepare for the night. Don't let yourself get exhausted.

LOST

If you think you're lost, it is usually best to stay in one place and wait to be found. (See "LOST" in Chapter 6.)

Direct your efforts to conserving energy and obtaining shelter and water. Limit your travel to getting to an open area where you can be seen from the air.

DIRECTION INDICATORS

The most reliable and practical direction-finding tool in the wild is a compass. The legendary Horace Kephart, in his book *Camping and Woodcraft,* published in 1916, spent some 12 to 15 pages exploring and explaining all the natural direction indicators that he had ever heard of and the scientific basis, if any, behind each. Kep's final statement about what really works? "Carry a compass."

Among the few natural direction indicators that are at all accurate and practical are the North Star, Orion's Belt, and the sun.

NORTH STAR

Find the constellation commonly called the Big Dipper.

An imaginary line from the two stars that form the lip of the dipper will point to the North Star which is almost exactly over true north.

ORION'S BELT

In the constellation Orion, the uppermost star of Orion's belt rises almost exactly in the east and sets almost due west. When Orion is overhead, however, it is not an accurate direction aid.

SOUTH BY A WATCH & THE SUN

(NORTHERN HEMISPHERE)
Point the hour hand of a watch toward the sun.

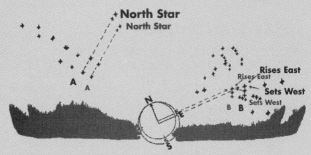

FIGURE 2.3–Nighttime Direction Indicators

A. NORTH STAR: A line through the two stars on the lip of the Big Dipper points to the north star. **B. ORION'S BELT:** The uppermost star in Orion's belt rises almost exactly in the east and sets almost exactly in the west.

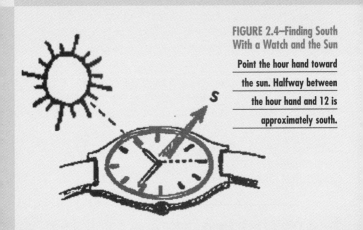

FIGURE 2.4–Finding South With a Watch and the Sun

Point the hour hand toward the sun. Halfway between the hour hand and 12 is approximately south.

TiME iNDiCATORS

Although the pressures placed on us by time schedules and deadlines in civilization make it tempting to ignore time in the wild, there are cases when checking the time can be very helpful. It's especially valuable in keeping track of how far and how fast you've traveled and planning when to stop for the night.

TiME BY A COMPASS

If you have no watch available, a compass can be used to estimate time.

Orient the compass to magnetic north and correct for declination.

Stand a straight twig on the edge of the compass rim and move it so its shadow falls across the hub of the compass needle.

The position of the shadow on the opposite rim of the compass, if north is assumed to be 12 o'clock, will be the approximate hour. This method is least accurate in the early morning and late afternoon.

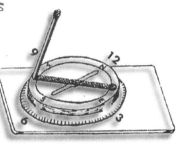

FIGURE 2.5–Estimating Time With a Compass

With the compass oriented to North, stand a stick on the rim so its shadow falls across the needle hub. Assuming North is 12, where the shadow crosses the opposite rim is the approximate hour.

TiME TO SUNSET

To estimate how long it will be until sunset, face the sun and hold your arm out straight toward the sun with your palm turned to face you. Count the number of finger-widths that can be seen between the horizon and the sun.

Each finger-width equals about 15 minutes until sunset.

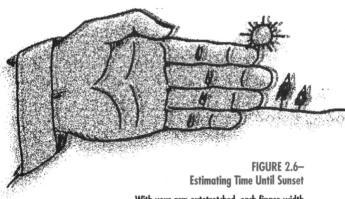

**FIGURE 2.6—
Estimating Time Until Sunset**

With your arm outstretched, each finger-width
between the horizon and the sun equals about fifteen minutes.

The Camper's Pocket Handbook

OBSERVATION

You're out there to see things, not to stare at your boots as you grunt along the trail or drop perspiration on the bow deck of your canoe as you grind out the miles. Stopping every now and then and looking backward is a wonderful navigation tool, right up there with "feeling" the sun on your body as you walk, noting vegetation changes, and remembering which way rivers are flowing. In a sense, you're fitting yourself into the territory that the map represents. It also helps to look ahead on the map and try to form a picture of where you are going. If you can do that, any discrepencies should jolt you out of your dreams and let you know that you just might be in the wrong place.

Soak up the country. That's why you're there in the first place!

3

WEATHER

Forecasting: Give It A Try!

For the most part, dealing with weather in the backcountry is simply a matter of taking what you get and doing the best you can. For planning the pace and activities of a trip, however, some effort at forecasting the weather in the field is worthwhile. You'll probably be only slightly less accurate than a professional meteorologist.

No single weather sign will give an accurate forecast, and at times some signs may seem contradictory. If you observe an overall trend over a period of time, however, you'll usually turn up with a pretty accurate forecast.

In the field, your observations are usually limited to watching clouds and the speed and direction of wind.

CLOUD OBSERVATIONS

Clouds are seldom of only one type and frequently are seen in changing combinations. Often the way that clouds develop and progress will be the key to what they mean.

CIRRUS: Detached, scattered wisps usually indicating good weather. If they're thickly bunched, however, it may mean rain within 24 hours.

CIRROCUMULUS: Thin, white rippled patches with some vertical development that may grow slightly during the day and disperse at night. They usually indicate good weather. Vertical growth continued into the late afternoon may lead to a brief shower or storm.

CIRROSTRATUS: A transparent, whitish film over all or part of the sky giving a "halo" effect around the sun. When followed by an approaching bank of altostratus, it indicates a warm front bringing rain in 12 to 14 hours.

ALTOSTRATUS: A grayish, uniform, striated cloud covering all or part of the sky, thin enough to vaguely see the sun. Usually means rain within 12 hours.

ALTOCUMULUS: An extensive sheet of white or gray cloudlets, sometimes in rows. Indicates unsettled weather or an approaching front.

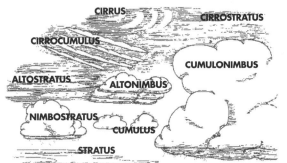

FIGURE 3.1–Cloud Formations

STRATUS: A low-lying gray layer with a uniform base that masks the sun, usually bringing drizzle or snow flurries.

NIMBOSTRATUS: A darker gray layer that completely blots out the sun. Usually brings continuous rain or snow.

CUMULUS: Fluffy white puffballs with flat bases and rounded sides and tops. Usually forecasts fair weather.

CUMULONIMBUS: Tall, massive thunderheads with a flat, dark bottom. A reliable indicator of heavy showers with possible thunderstorms or hail.

FOG: A stratus cloud at ground level. If generated at night, will usually disappear in the morning and indicates fair weather. If generated during the day, indicates an approaching storm system.

The Camper's Pocket Handbook

WIND

Wind direction is the direction the wind is coming from. A breeze that is going from west to east is a west wind.

Wind is often an indicator of the movement of high and low pressure areas since the winds around each spin in opposite directions. For that reason, some oversimplified but useful generalizations can be made about wind direction and weather.

NORTH WINDS are usually brisk and cool.

EAST WINDS are common in a storm, and may progress to north or northeast with increased and prolonged rain or snow.

SOUTH WINDS in summer often precede rain. Winter south winds may bring cold rains or a mid-winter thaw.

WEST WINDS usually bring fair weather.

WIND CHILL

Depending on your mode of travel, the speed of the wind may have a profound effect on your progress or activities. When wind is combined with cold a "wind chill" factor is created and is dramatically important because of the increased cooling effect on the body. The "Triple Threat" combination of wind, cold, and water (wet clothing) makes the body cool so much faster that it can quickly become a dire emergency if you're unprepared.

WIND CHILL FACTOR

Wind Speed Temperature (F)

MPH	50	40	30	10	0	-10	-20	-30	-40
	WIND CHILL								
5	48	37	27	16	7	-5	-15	-26	-36
10	40	28	16	4	-9	-21	-33	-46	-58
15	36	22	9	-5	-18	-36	-45	-58	-72
20	32	18	4	-10	-25	-39	-53	-67	-82
25	30	16	0	-15	-29	-44	-59	-74	-88
30	28	13	-2	-18	-33	-48	-63	-79	-94
35	27	11	-4	-20	-35	-49	-67	-82	-98
40	26	10	-6	-21	-37	-53	-69	-85	-100

little danger if properly clothed	severe frostbite danger to exposed flesh	extreme freezing danger

FIGURE 3.2

WIND SPEED

A modified version of the Beaufort Wind Speed Scale provides a reference for estimating wind speed in the field.

WIND SPEED SCALE

MPH	Description / Indications
0-1	Calm Smoke rises vertically
1-7	Slight Breeze Wind direction shown by smoke but not by waves.
8-12	Gentle Breeze Wind felt on face, leaves rustle, some small waves.
13-18	Moderate Breeze Dust, loose papers blow, small branches move.
19-24	Fresh Breeze Small trees in leaf sway.
25-31	Strong Breeze Large branches in motion.
	(Avoid water travel if wind speed is above this level.)
32-38	Moderate Gale Whole trees in motion
39-46	Fresh Gale Twigs break off trees, walking is impeded.
47-54	Strong Gale Tree limbs break off.
55-63	Whole Gale Trees uprooted.
64-72	Storm Widespread damage.
73+	Hurricane

FIGURE 3.3

FOLKLORE RHYMES

Over hundreds of years of
casual weather obser-
vation, many rhymes
and sayings have
evolved to describe what weather
can be expected from certain signs. While some
are of little value, a few are relatively reliable.

Evening red, morning gray, sends the traveler on his way;
Evening gray, morning red, stays the traveler home in bed.

> *When the dew is on the grass,*
> > *rain will rarely come to pass;*
> *When the dew at morn is gone,*
> > *rain will come before too long.*

> *Rainbow in the morning,*
> > *shepherds take warning;*
> *Rainbow at night,*
> > *shepherd's delight.*
> *Rainbow to windward,*
> > *foul fall the day;*
> *Rainbow to leeward,*
> > *damp runs away.*

The Camper's Pocket Handbook

STORMS

The rapid development of a storm can present a serious potential danger if you fail to take the signs of the storm seriously and don't prepare yourself to ride out the blow. Ignore the signs of an approaching storm at your own risk.

Thunderstorms generally approach from the west or northwest and move east or southeast. A distant storm, if it appears to the north, south, or east, may miss your position.

In general, thunderstorms develop from cumulus clouds that grow vertically, forming an "anvil top" and a dark underside. The distance and speed of a storm can be estimated by the sound of the thunder, which travels about one mile every 5 seconds. Count the seconds between the lightning flash and thunder. Divide the number of seconds by 5 to get the approximate distance of the storm in miles.

Lightning will usually strike prominent, exposed

objects. The safest position to camp in a storm is usually at low elevation where there are no prominent high points. A good example is an evenly forested valley. Avoid exposed peaks, open bodies of water, or any large clearings.

A relatively safe area exists around tall, prominent objects. The safe area, often called the "Cone of Protection," extends from near, but not next to, the base of the object out to where a 45 degree angle from the top of the object would meet the ground. If you must wait out a storm in an exposed area, try to get within the Cone of Protection formed by a tree or cliff.

If you're in a tent, wear your boots and squat on the floor or sit on a foam pad with your knees drawn up to minimize your exposure to ground currents that may radiate along the ground from a nearby lightning strike.

Don't Forget Your Veggies!

When, what kind and how much food and water you eat in the wild can mean the difference between enjoying a difficult trip, being tired and miserable, or not surviving at all. Without the proper fuel your body cannot sustain work, provide bursts of energy, maintain temperature, or heal and rebuild tissue.

FOOD TYPES

A proper balance of calories from carbohydrates, fats and proteins must be maintained.

Each gram of carbohydrate produces about 4 calories of energy that is available relatively quickly after eating. Carbohydrates require less energy and water for digestion than do fats and proteins, which makes them the best food to eat when supplies are limited. About 50 percent of the diet should be carbohydrates. Primary sources of carbohydrates are breads, cereals, pasta, honey, jam, fruits, and candy.

Fats are the most efficient food, producing about 9 calories per gram. The quantity of fat in the diet is normally about 20 percent to 25 percent. Fats are especially valuable in cold conditions or when physical exertion is extreme. The best sources of fat (most calories per pound) are margarine and cooking oil. Other sources are nuts, peanut butter, cheese, bacon, and sausage.

Protein produces about 4 calories per gram. Only about 70 grams (2.4 ox.) of protein are needed per day. The inclusion of dried milk with cereal, jerky, or some freeze-dried meat will provide all the protein necessary for a wilderness trip.

CALORIE REQUIREMENTS

Most adults require 2200 to 2700 calories per day. On a wilderness trip about 1000 to 1500 extra calories per day are usually sufficient. The backcountry isn't the place for a crash diet.

TIMING OF MEALS

The often-advised method of constantly eating small amounts while traveling in the wild is practiced by many but is not, in fact, the most efficient method of fueling the body. While there is a substantial psychological boost from frequent snacking, especially just before a strenuous task, there is virtually no physical benefit. The food eaten does not have time to provide additional energy and the body is forced to spend energy for digestion while also trying to spend energy on travel. At times, however, the psychological benefit may outweigh the energy expense.

WATER REQUIREMENTS

Of all the requirements for body function, water is second only to oxygen. It is virtually impossible to take in too much water while traveling in the wild.

The food that you normally eat in a day contains about a quart of water. Most people drink a quart and a half of water in various forms each day. In the wild, however, your fluid needs increase tremendously even though you may not feel more thirsty. Sweating alone may increase your total daily fluid needs to a gallon or more.

In cold weather, fluid loss is often every bit as great as in warm weather, even though it may not be obvious as sweat. You lose a great deal of water through respiration and other factors. Your thirst mechanism, however, is less acute in the cold: so you may not feel thirsty even when your body needs fluid.

Drinking water or other fluids on any trip in the

wild, but especially in the cold, must be a constant habit whether you feel thirsty or not. A good rule of thumb is to drink water or some other beverage at every rest and snack break.

Your urine output is a valuable indicator of fluid levels in the body. Normal urination should occur 3 to 4 times a day, and the urine should be clear to light yellow. Less frequent urination, darker urine, or less volume of urine indicates that fluid intake should be increased. If you notice these changes, start drinking more water right away until things return to normal.

WATER SOURCES

The safest water is usually from a purified municipal water supply and must be carried into the wild. At about 8 pounds a gallon, however, it's not practical to carry much water with you. You must use water sources in the wild to replenish your supply.

The preferred sources of water in the wild are moving streams or springs that flow from areas where there are no people and few animals. Avoid water sources downstream of or near settlements, towns, farms fields, or livestock areas.

When possible, gather water that has little sediment and is from a source that is moving rather than stagnant. If no streams are available, try to get lake or pond water from as deep as possible, since most of the debris floats on the surface and much of the bacteria stays near the surface.

When you can collect it, rain water is usually pretty clean but should still be purified since air pollutants may be picked up by the rain.

Snow and ice may be used as sources of water if you have the time, patience, and fuel to melt them. It takes a surprisingly large amount of snow to make a useful amount of water. While melted snow and ice are usually relatively clean, purification is still advisable for the same reason as rainwater.

To melt snow for water, use very low heat and start with some leftover water in a large pan, adding small bits of snow at a time. With too little water to start with, snow can scorch and impart a disagreeable taste to the water. The old joke about somebody not being able to boil water without burning it isn't funny to winter campers.

SOLAR STILL

In a pinch, and if you have the time, you can construct a solar still to gather water even in the driest of areas. Said to be the greatest advancement in survival techniques since World War II, the solar still is relatively easy to build with materials usually available to wilderness travelers.

MATERIALS

Container—best is a wide plastic bowl or bucket, but others can be used.

A 6-foot-square sheet of clear plastic—as thin as possible with no holes. (1 mil thick is best, 3-4 mil is adequate)

Plastic tubing 4' to 6' long—for use as an extended "straw" to draw water without disassembling the still. (Not essential, but helpful.)

PROCEDURE

1. Locate a suitable site. A sandy wash is best. An alternative is any depression where rain might normally collect. Look for fine soil and constant exposure to direct sunlight.
2. Dig hole 40" wide, with sides that go straight down 20", then taper to a central cavity.
3. Place the container in the middle of the central cavity.

4. Secure one end of the tubing in the container, run the other end up and out of the hole, and secure to keep clean and open.
5. Drape the plastic sheet over the hole and anchor with soil or rocks around all edges.
6. Push center of sheet down to an inverted cone with sides about 25 to 40 degrees from horizontal. Plastic should be about 2" to 4" above the soil in hole and touch soil only at the rim. Place a small rock or weight in center of cone to hold it down, immediately over the center of the container.
7. Seal all edges of the plastic with extra soil to ensure no air can pass under the sheet.
8. In one to two hours, the air and soil under the sheet will heat and moisture will condense on the plastic sheet. As droplets form, they will run down the inverted cone and drip off the point into the container.

The water from the distilling process will be almost perfectly pure. The only potential for contamination may be from very alkaline soil that may be carried by water droplets from the rim to the container. If this occurs, raise the sheet off the rim with rocks and seal behind them with soil.

Water may be sucked directly from the container using the plastic tubing as a straw. Opening the still to retrieve the water will stop the production, and it will have to start over when the still is re-sealed.

Production of the still can be boosted by increasing the humidity in the still. Place cut plant material on the bottom of the hole with moist inner surfaces exposed, but not touching the plastic. Plants used for this should have high moisture content such as cactus.

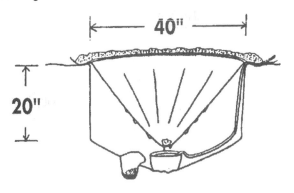

FIGURE 4.1-Solar Still

Yield from a solar still may be 1 to 3 quarts per day.

Further boosting of the still humidity is possible with a waste trough dug 4"-5" deep and a foot long near the bottom of the hole. Waste fluids, including urine, can be discarded there and help produce more pure water.

Yield from a solar still is 1 to 3 quarts of water per day. Constructing another still will yield more total water than one bigger one will.

WATER PURIFICATION

Virtually all natural water sources should be considered polluted to some extent. Water purifying is easy. It's simply not worth the risk of getting sick and ruining your trip by not purifying your water.

Heating water to at least 150 degrees is probably the bare minimum that is needed to make water drinkable, but boiling for 5 minutes is preferred and is by far the most effective purification method.

Either iodine or chlorine tablets may also be used to purify water. The effectiveness of iodine and chlorine may be reduced, however, by very cold water or water with lots of sediment.

Filters may be used for some purification, to clarify muddy waters and remove some of the taste left from iodine purification.

Naturally, all of the water you drink or cook with must be purified, but don't forget that the final rinse after washing dishes should be with purified water. Remember too, in case of injury, to only wash wounds with purified water.

EMERGENCY FOODS

Emergency foods are those that you take along (preferably) or find in the wild (if you have no other choice) and eat when other food supplies are dwindling or unavailable.

EMERGENCY FOODS CARRIED ALONG

Some of the foods you normally use as staples are excellent for emergency use as well. It is always wise to carry an extra ration or two of these for each week of trip that is planned, to be able to keep fed and functioning if the trip is delayed beyond the planned timetable.

Among the best emergency foods are trail mix or GORP, nuts, dried fruit, beef jerky, chocolate, granola bars.

EMERGENCY FOODS FOUND IN THE WILD

With the popularity of many of the backpacking, camping, climbing and canoeing areas in North America, it's no longer appropriate to gather wild foods unless faced with an emergency.

In a survival or near-survival situation, however, the choice to supplement food supplies with edible plants and animals may not be the best use of the limited energy available because the gathering of the food may use more calories than the food can provide.

WILD EDIBLE CALORIE CONTENT:

Calories per pound (Edible part before cooking)

FISH

Bass	472
Carp	522
Catfish, Freshwater	467
Pike, Walleye	422
Salmon, King	1007
Trout, Rainbow	885

MEAT, FOWL & SHELLFISH

Clams	363
Crab, Saltwater	422
Crayfish, Freshwater	327
Duck	613
Eggs, average (Duck, Goose)	700
Rabbit	490
Turtle, Green	404
Venison, Lean	572

BERRIES

Blackberries	250
Blueberries	259
Grapes, American	178
Raspberries, Black	321

NUTS - SHELLED

Beechnuts	2576
Hickory Nuts	3053
Pine Nuts, Pinyon	2880
Walnuts, Black	2849

OTHER PLANTS

Dandelion Greens	204

* Adapted from *Mountain Wilderness Survival*, by Craig E. Patterson, And/Or Press, Berkeley, California, 1979

FIGURE 4.2-Wild Edibles Calorie Content

When trying to stay alive, rest and use your energy only for making shelter, staying warm, and finding water. It is possible to survive many days without food, but water is a necessity for even short-term survival.

The gathering of plants and methods of killing animals described below are illegal in many places and frequently inhumane. If, however, your survival must be long term, there may be no other choice.

EDIBLE PLANTS

BERRIES: The most easily recognizable plant foods are berries. Strawberries, blueberries, blackberries, and raspberries are easily found when in season.

PINE NUTS: Available in virtually all cone-bearing trees, some nuts may be too small to be useful. Very large cones usually have nuts large enough to be worth harvesting. *Pick an unopened cone* off the tree; scorch it over a fire to burn off some of the exterior pitch and partially roast the nuts. *Smash the cone* lengthwise between rocks to split it open so it can be torn apart and the nuts removed. *The pine nuts* can be further heated in a dry pan to remove the turpentine-like taste.

ACORNS: Nearly all acorns contain very bitter tasting tannic acid. The tannic acid can be removed by soaking in water for several hours or by boiling crushed acorns for 1 hour in three changes of water.

DANDELIONS: Common and easily recognized and found, dandelion leaves and greens from the base of the plant can be eaten raw if it is early in the season before the flower blooms. After the dandelion flower blooms, the roots and greens may be boiled briefly in 2 or 3 changes of water to remove the bitter taste. Either way, they are excellent as a salad.

FIDDLEHEADS (BRACKEN FERN): The young curled shoots may be eaten raw or boiled until tender in salted water and eaten like asparagus.

CAT-TAILS: Useful year-round, virtually all parts that are not too dry or stringy are edible. Tender sprouts in spring may be eaten raw. Top brown spike may be boiled and eaten like corn-on-the-cob. Root parts are similar to potatoes and can be used like potatoes or as an addition to salad. Stalk may be peeled and the white inner portion of the stem eaten raw.

EDIBLE CREATURES

Far less appealing than other wild foods, eating wild creatures will require a stronger stomach, more desperation and a good deal more work to catch and prepare for eating.

GRASSHOPPERS: Eat raw if you are very hungry. The wings can be pulled off to ease swallowing.

GRUBS (WHITE INSECT LARVAE): Also require great

willpower to eat. Can be found under moist leaf mulch in damp woods. Can be eaten raw or cut the heads off and boil or broil.

FRESHWATER CLAMS AND MUSSELS: Choose only those that are in clean water, alive, and quick to slam shut when disturbed. May be boiled or steamed open.

EGGS: All kinds are edible and may be cooked like chicken eggs.

GROUND SQUIRRELS: Fairly easy to catch. Will nearly always emerge from hole 10 to 15 minutes after being chased in. Catch with snare loop around hole. Can also use a #8 or #10 treble hook laid just below hole entrance with line run around back of hole. When squirrel emerges, yank line and snag it with the hook. Cut off head, gut, and skin. Roast, broil or fry.

RABBITS: Harder to catch, but possible with wire snare along trail. Very tasty but very lean. Arctic explorer Vilhjalmur Stefansson said a diet of rabbit alone would lead to "rabbit starvation" due to lack of fat in an environment where a high fat diet was needed for survival.

PORCUPINES: Slow and easy to chase down and kill with a club. Watch for bark-stripped tree trunks with sausage shaped manure droppings 1" to 1½" long nearby. If manure is fresh, porcupine is still close.

The belly has no quills, so gut and skin like other small animals.

FiSHiNG

If fishing gear is not available makeshift equipment is relatively easy to improvise.

The most productive fishing areas in the wild are usually in the eddies at the base of falls and rapids. If not successful at first, a simple variation of the fishing depth may produce results.

CATChiNG COMMON FiSH

WALLEYE: Called walleyed pike in the midwest, pickerel in Canada and pike perch in the east, it is usually found fairly deep. Use a bright artificial spinner or a minnow. Let it bump along the bottom. (Anticipate snags.) May also be found deep in lakes. Spawns when water is 38 to 44 degrees, usually in shallow riffles in streams or on shallow gravel reefs in lakes.

NORTHERN PIKE: Called jackfish in Canada, it is common at the foot of rapids and falls as well as where a stream empties into a larger river or a lake. May be hard to find in a lake, but possible near shore and underwater fallen trees. Use a shiny spoon or spinner and fish shallower than for the walleye. Northerns spawn immediately after the ice melt in spring, usually in small streams or grassy lake margins.

LAKE TROUT: Found in very cold and deep northern lakes. Right after the thaw, troll shallow. Later in the season, troll deeper. Following the cold water, in June they may be at 30 feet while in July they may go down to 50 to 70 feet. Use a spoon, minnow or piece of fish for best results.

SUNFISH FAMILY: *BASS, SUNFISH, CRAPPIE:* Abundant in southern lakes with thick vegetation. Found near lily pads, rocky projections or logs. Use worms, small minnows or a spinner.

FASTWATER TROUT AND SALMON: In spring during spawning, they are found flocking upstream. Usually respond to spinners as well as flies.

MINNOWS: In a pinch, a net such as a mosquito head-net may be used to trap minnows which can be boiled or fried and eaten whole. Netting is illegal in most areas.

FISH PREPARATION

CLEANING

One method of cleaning fish is simply to cut off the head, tail and fins, slice down the belly, and gut it. Scales can be scraped off.

Many people prefer to fillet the fish, which is less messy and, with practice, faster. First, cut downward behind the gills from spine. Then, slice alongside the backbone, slowly working the meat away from the ribs, peeling it off in one piece on each side. Avoid cutting into the abdominal cavity. Skin can then be sliced off, leaving two slabs of nearly boneless meat (depending on the fish) and all the garbage in one piece.

FRYING

Most common method used, but fried fish gets tiresome after several days. Use plenty of oil and a hot skillet. The fish may be breaded or not with cracker crumbs, flour, or cornmeal.

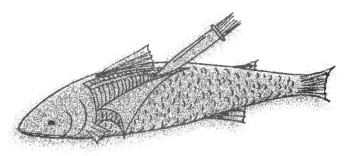

FIGURE 4.3-Fish Fillet Technique

Carefully slice along the backbone

and ribs to remove all the meat.

COOK ON A STICK

Fish that have been gutted can be poked on a stick and roasted over an open fire. Eating is messy but preparation is fast and requires no utensils.

BROILING

A pleasant alternative to frying is broiling in foil. Place the fillets in heavy tin foil. Add margarine and a selection of spices to taste, wrap well, and place in the coals of an open fire for 15 to 20 minutes. Spices may include dried onion, lemon crystals, pepper, oregano, and garlic.

STOVE SAFETY

The greatest key to safe stove operation is to know the operation and repair of your stove thoroughly and check it carefully before the trip. The following stove safety rules are important to prevent problems.

1. Carry fuel only in containers designed to be carried in a pack in the wild.

2. Check the stove tank temperature frequently. It should always be cool enough to touch.

3. Do not re-fuel or re-light a hot stove. Fill the tank before starting a meal.

4. Fill the tank only ¾ full to allow room for the fuel to expand and vaporize.

5 . Use only fuel for which the stove was made.

6 . Do not start a stove inside a tent or confined space.

7 . Set stove on a firm, level surface that cannot warp or melt.

8 . Do not use over-sized pot or enclose the stove with foil to increase heat. The increased heat may overheat the tank. Use only the windscreen designed for the stove! A windbreak set up a couple of feet away is okay, though.

9 . Be sure to have sufficient ventilation. A closed tent is **NOT** sufficiently ventilated. Carbon monoxide poisoning is almost unnoticeable when it starts, and it can happen far more easily at altitude. Be alert for headache, dizziness or nausea and act fast to get to fresh air.

10. If the stove is suddenly engulfed in flame due to spilled fuel, the fire must be put out quickly or it may overheat the tank. Try to shut off the fuel flow and smother the flames with dirt. Do not throw water on it. The water will only spread the burning fuel elsewhere.

11. If the stove has a safety valve and the stove

becomes overheated or over pressurized, the valve may suddenly release a spray of fuel. The spray of fuel will probably ignite immediately. Do not try to extinguish a burning jet of fuel from a safety valve. Aim the jet of flame in a safe direction and wait for it to burn itself out.

MEDICAL PROBLEMS

Be Safe–Learn the Basics!

NOTE: The following information is only a rough guideline to remind you how to treat certain medical problems in the wild. Before you leave civilization, you owe it to yourself, your companions, and those that will be waiting for you to return to study and learn basic first aid techniques and take a class in cardio-pulmonary resuscitation (CPR).

The medical problems that you'll face in the backcountry are usually relatively minor and only make the trip uncomfortable. Some of them, however, could become serious and potentially threaten survival if not treated properly.

UNCONScioUS PATiENTS

If a person is unconscious after a sudden injury or illness, you must act immediately! If the person is awake and alert you have time to examine him and think about the proper treatment.

An unconscious patient cannot keep his airway open and cannot tell you what's wrong. Regardless of the cause of the unconsciousness, you must assume that the worst has happened and do a fast examination to see if artificial respiration is needed.*

1. **POSITION THE VICTIM ON BACK**
2. **OPEN AIRWAY** (Use Head Tilt/Chin Lift)
3. **CHECK FOR BREATHING**
4. **LOOK** across the chest for movement, **LISTEN** over the mouth for air movement and **FEEL** air movement on the side of your face.
5. **PERFORM ARTIFICIAL RESPIRATION**. Give two quick, full breaths, allowing exhalation between. Open the patient's airway, pinch his nose closed, seal your mouth over patient's mouth, exhale strongly until the patient's chest rises, remove your mouth, and allow patient to exhale. Repeat once every 5 seconds.

*(Adapted from the Journal of the American Medical Association Vol 255, No. 21 June 6, 1986)

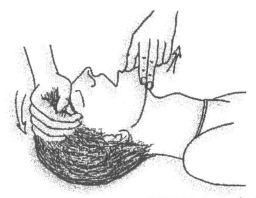

FIGURE 5.1–Opening the Airway (Head Tilt/Chin Lift)

Push down on the forehead to tilt the head back, and lift the chin upward.

6. **CHECK FOR A PULSE**

7. **PERFORM CHEST COMPRESSIONS WITH ARTIFICIAL RESPIRATION (CPR)** Perform chest compressions and rescue breathing in cycles of 15 compressions followed by 2 breaths. After four cycles of 15 compressions and 2 breaths, recheck for absence of breathing and pulse. Continue until you are either relieved by another rescuer, the patient revives, or you are too exhausted to continue.

**FIGURE 5.2–
CPR Hand Position**

When doing chest

compressions, apply

pressure only on the

lower third of the

breast bone.

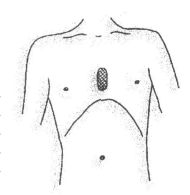

CHOKING EMERGENCIES

Choking on a piece of food can quickly kill an otherwise healthy person by blocking the airway and making breathing impossible. The treatment is easy and effective if applied soon enough.

IF THE PERSON CAN SPEAK OR COUGH:

Do nothing.

His own efforts to cough are better than anything you can do to help. Prepare to help if the person becomes unable to speak or cough.

Apply abdominal thrusts (Heimlich Maneuver)

1. Stand behind the person and place your arms around his chest.

2. Place your left fist against his abdomen half-way between his navel and lower edge of his rib cage. Place your right hand on your left fist.

3. Quickly and abruptly, thrust inward and upward against the patient's abdomen four times.

4. Repeat the abdominal thrusts until the object he is choking on comes out.

SHOCK IN THE INJURED PATIENT

Shock is usually the result of a profound loss of body fluid. The fluid lost is usually blood, but it may also be fluid lost through second or third degree burns or the fluid lost through vomiting or diarrhea.

SIGNS OF SHOCK (Not all may be present)

1. Pulse is fast. (120 per minute or more)
2. Breathing is fast. (24 to 36 times per minute)

3. Skin is pale, cool and clammy.
4. The patient is usually anxious and may be confused.

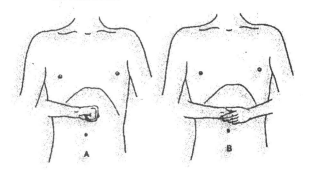

FIGURE 5.3–Heimlich Maneuver Hand Placement

A. Reaching around the patient from behind,

place your right fist between his navel and rib cage.

B. Then place your left hand over your right fist

and thrust inward and upward.

SHOCK TREATMENT IN THE WILD

1. Stop any external bleeding with direct pressure on the wound.
2. Have the patient rest and keep him warm.
3. Raise the patient's feet and legs to about a

45 degree angle to encourage blood flow to the vital organs. (Do not do this if a head injury is involved, or if there is a possible broken leg or hip.)

4. Splint any broken bones.
5. Evacuate as rapidly as possible.
6. Give the patient frequent small quantities of fluid by mouth as tolerated.

CHEST PAIN

The chest pain of a heart attack usually feels crushing or heavy and starts in the center or left side of the chest and may radiate to the neck, left arm, or jaw. Sweating, nausea, and shortness of breath may also be present.

Any patient with a suspected heart attack must rest completely with no exertion. Aspirin may help the pain and the blood thinning properties of aspirin may help the blood flow to the heart. Evacuate as soon as possible with an absolute minimum of physical exertion by the patient.

HEAD INJURIES

If the patient is unconscious after a head injury, even for a brief time, some brain injury has occurred.

If the patient wakes up after only a minute or two and slowly regains all his normal faculties, no further travel should be attempted, and the patient should rest for at least 24 hours. After that, he should be able to travel carefully.

If the patient remains unconscious or if the patient wakes up and then lapses back into unconsciousness, there may be bleeding within the skull and the patient should be evacuated immediately.

If any headache or nausea after a head injury lasts more than 2 hours or if any confusion lasts more than 15 minutes, the patient should be evacuated.

SKIN WOUNDS

LACERATIONS, ABRASIONS, PUNCTURES

Stop bleeding with direct pressure on the wound.

A sterile dressing is preferred against the wound, but a bandanna, shirt, or even a bare hand is sufficient.

Hold firm pressure for at least 5 minutes for mild bleeding, and 10 minutes for serious bleeding.

CLEAN THE WOUND

Wash thoroughly with soap and gentle scrubbing. Proper cleaning will probably re-start some minor bleeding. The speed and ease of healing is directly related to how clean the wound is.

Puncture wounds should be allowed or encouraged to bleed a little to help clean the inside of the wound.

Clean lacerations should be closed with wound closure tape strips or butterfly bandages made from tape. Wound closure strips should be set about one-quarter to one-half inch apart to bring the edges of the wound back together in a normal position.

Do not close wounds that are not thoroughly clean or that may be particularly prone to infection such as animal bites. The wound will heal without being closed but will take longer and may leave a larger scar.

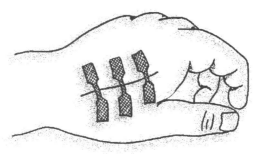

FIGURE 5.4-Butterfly Bandage

Stick one end of the bandage next to the wound, pull the wound

edges together and stick down the other end of the bandage.

The wound edges should just meet in a normal position.

APPLY DRESSING

A thin layer of antibiotic ointment may be applied to the wound and a sterile dressing placed over the wound and secured in place with tape or a bandage.

Keep the dressing as dry as possible. Dressings should be changed if they get wet or dirty.

INFECTED WOUNDS

Signs of infection include increasing tenderness, redness, and/or swelling around the wound. Pockets of pus may develop in the wound which must be drained. Warm soaks for 15 minutes, 4 times a day, will help bring the infection to a head. Wound closure tapes may have to be removed and the wound allowed to open and drain. Infected punctures should be coaxed open after soaking and allowed to drain. Do not tape the wound closed after draining. Clean it again and apply antibiotic ointment and a sterile dressing.

SPLINTER REMOVAL

Clean the area around the splinter. Use a needle, pin, or tip of a small knife blade sterilized in a flame to remove the skin over the splinter. Expose enough of the end of the splinter to allow a good grasp with the tweezers. Grasp the splinter firmly and pull it straight

The Camper's Pocket Handbook

out in the opposite direction that it went in to avoid breaking it off.

A blister is best treated while it is still a "hot spot," before a bubble forms. Place a ring of moleskin bandage or tape in a circle around the hot spot. Cover with a bandage to keep pressure and friction off the blister. If you have it, Spenco Second Skin is an excellent blister dressing.

A fully developed blister should be drained only if further activity is likely to break it open. Clean the entire blister. Use a needle, pin, or the tip of a small knife blade sterilized in a flame to pierce the blister near the base and allow it to drain. Do not remove the skin over the blister for 3 to 5 days. Clean the

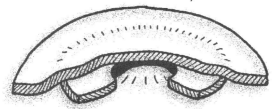

FIGURE 5.5-Moleskin Ring

Cut a ring of moleskin and place it around the blister. Cover with another

piece of moleskin or a bandage to keep pressure and friction off the blister.

MEDICAL PROBLEMS   97

area and place a moleskin ring and bandage over it.

If the blister ruptures and the skin over it is partially torn off, gently trim away the loose tissue, clean the wound and apply antibiotic ointment and a sterile dressing. Apply a moleskin ring to avoid pressure and chafing.

FISHHOOK INJURIES

Impaled fishhooks should be removed unless they are in the face or where removal might be difficult or may damage other structures.

If the hook is to be left in, clean the area and secure the hook in place with tape.

PUSH THROUGH - CLIP OFF TECHNIQUE

Clean the skin around the hook, especially where the point will come out when it is pushed through. Use a pair of pliers or similar tool to get a good grip on the hook. Forcefully shove the hook in one firm thrust the rest of the way through the skin so the barb comes out. (This often takes more force than you may expect and will be quite painful.) The barb should be clipped off with side-cutting pliers and the remaining hook backed out the way it went in. (Cup your hand over the pliers when clipping the barb off in case the clipped off portion of the hook flies up.)

An embedded hook may be removed with a length of stout twine or fish line tied into about a 10-inch loop. Loop the line over the hook and hold it along the skin in the opposite direction that the shank of the hook is pointing. Press the top of the hook straight down onto the skin to disengage the barb. Quickly pull back on the loop along the surface of the skin to pull the hook out the way it went in.

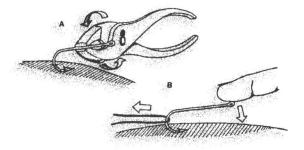

FIGURE 5.6-Fishhook Removal

A. Push Through - Clip Off. Force the hook the rest of the way through the skin in one motion. Clip off the barb and back the hook out.

B. String Technique. Push down on the top of the hook to disengage the barb and pull back quickly with the string along the surface of the skin.

BURNS

First degree burns, like sunburn, are superficial, red, and painful. Cool the burn with water and keep it clean. It should heal in about 48 hours.

Second degree burns are usually red, blistered, and very painful.

Third degree burns involve the full thickness of the skin. They may be charred or white, usually dry, and often painless because the nerves in the area have been destroyed.

If a hand or arm is burned, remove all rings and watches immediately. Swelling under rings or watches may cause restriction of blood flow. Clean the burn well with soap and clean water. Do not open blisters. Apply antibiotic ointment to any blisters that open on their own. Apply dry sterile dressings to the burns. Immobilize and elevate burned extremities. Change dressings every 2 days or anytime they get wet or dirty. Give pain medication as needed.

EYE PROBLEMS

FOREIGN BODY IN THE EYE

Close the eye and allow tears to wash the object out. Do not rub the eye. The eye may be flushed with eye drops to help wash the object out. Objects you can see may be very gently coaxed to the inner corner of the eye with a clean cotton swab or corner of a tissue. If the object does not move when the eye blinks, it may be impossible to remove without professional help. Patch the eye and evacuate. If movement of the eye causes pain, patch both eyes to keep them still.

EYE INFECTION

An eye infection often feels like a foreign object or a "scratchy" sensation. The white portion of the eye may be reddened, and pus may be found in the inner corner. The eye may be stuck shut in the morning with dried pus. Warm soaks will open an eye stuck shut by dried pus.

Eye infections will usually resolve in 1 to 2 weeks with only treatment for pain. However, a serious situation may exist and evacuation may be necessary if:

1. The pupil does not constrict in response to light.

2. There is a cloudy appearance to the iris and pupil.

2. The white part of the eye is redder close to the iris and whiter away from the iris. (In minor infections it is opposite: red away from the iris and white near it.)

HYPOTHERMIA (EXPOSURE)

Hypothermia may occur slowly from exposure to cool, damp, and windy conditions or rapidly, as from a fall into cold water. If the combined temperatures of the air and water add up to less than 100 degrees, the hypothermia danger from immersion is severe. The hallmark symptoms of hypothermia are uncontrollable shivering and sluggish thinking.

Hypothermia is common in damp and windy conditions even when air temperatures are well above freezing. Fatigue is a major contributing factor, and it may also mask some of the symptoms. The key to dealing with hypothermia is to suspect it early and act fast to get the victim warm.

HYPOTHERMIA SYMPTOMS

Core	Temperature Symptoms
98–96	Intense and uncontrollable shivering. Unable to perform complex tasks.
95–91	Persistent violent shivering, with difficulty speaking, and sluggish thinking.
90–86	Shivering decreases, muscles become rigid. Exposed skin is blue or puffy. Poor coordination. Memory loss, incoherence, confusion, irrationality.
85–81	Drifting into stupor. Severe muscular rigidity. Dilation of pupils. Slow pulse and erratic respiration.
80–78	Unconsciousness, no reflexes, erratic heartbeat.
78 & Below	Pulmonary edema, heart and respiratory failure. Death.

FIGURE 5.7

Get the patient into shelter away from wind and wet conditions. Remove all wet clothing if possible. Protect the patient from further cooling. If possible, place the patient near a large roaring fire.

If no fire is possible, place stripped patient in a sleeping bag with a stripped rescuer in the bag also with skin-to-skin contact to provide additional warmth. Others may huddle around the patient and rescuer in the sleeping bag as close as possible to add body heat. If the patient is not much warmer in an hour or two, warm stones or warm water bottles should be placed in the sleeping bag at the patient's groin and sides of his chest to provide additional heat.

FROSTBITE

Frostbite is identified by skin that is pale, cold, and firm, with pain or numbness in the part. If it is possible that the part may re-freeze before evacuation is completed, do not try to thaw the part. Thawing and re-freezing causes disastrous damage. If the feet are frozen, thawing them will force the patient to travel only by stretcher. While they are frozen he still may be able to walk and do little further damage.

Frostbite should be re-warmed by immersion in warm water (110 degrees) for 20 to 30 minutes. Continue soaking until all portions are pink or burgundy red. If a warm-water bath is impossible, the

The Camper's Pocket Handbook

frostbitten part may be placed against the bare skin of another person's chest or abdomen until the pink color returns.

Aspirin is recommended for pain relief. When thawed, painful blisters may form. Apply loose sterile dressings, immobilize the frostbitten parts, and evacuate as soon as possible.

HEAT EXHAUSTION

Heat exhaustion is a form of shock caused by fluid depletion from excessive sweating. The patient is sweaty, pale, and weak. Skin is cool and clammy, and there may be dizziness, nausea, or vomiting. Have the patient rest in a cool place and give him plenty of fluids.

HEAT STROKE

The patient with heat stroke will have hot, dry skin, with no sweating. He may be confused and may quickly lose consciousness. The patient's temperature may rise rapidly to over 105 degrees, and death may be imminent unless he is rapidly cooled. This is a severe emergency, and you must act quickly to save his life!

Remove his clothes, pour cool water over him and fan him to hasten the cooling process. Continue cooling the patient until his temperature is down to about 101 degrees. Evacuate as soon as possible while periodically rechecking his temperature. Even after the patient feels better, he may suddenly get worse again.

Acute Mountain Sickness (AMS)

AMS usually occurs over 10,000 feet (3,000 meters), with rapid development of headache, weakness, nausea, vomiting, and shortness of breath. Descend at least to 6,500 feet (2,000 meters) in-crease fluid and carbohydrate intake, and restrict salt.

High Altitude Pulmonary Edema (HAPE)

Rare below 8,000 feet (2,500 meters), HAPE develops slowly over 1 to 3 days with shortness of breath, weakness, rapid heart rate, headache, and fever. As HAPE progresses, fluid builds in the lungs causing chest congestion and cough. Descend rapidly, increase fluid intake, and restrict salt.

Cerebral Edema (CE)

Rare below 11,000 feet (3,500 meters), symptoms of CE include severe headache, confusion, hallucinations, unstable walking, loss of vision and dexterity, and paralysis of facial muscles. Rapid descent is vital for survival.

BiTES & STiNGS

All bites have a high risk of infection. Bite wounds should be washed immediately and an antiseptic or even alcohol in the form of whiskey should be flushed through the wound. Bite wounds should not be closed with butterfly bandages or wound closure tapes. Apply a sterile dressing and observe for infection.

STINGS *(Bees, Wasps, Hornets, Yellow Jackets)*

The stings of all these pests produce instant pain and varying amounts of swelling. If a stinger is still in the skin, scrape it off with the edge of a knife. A normal sting reaction consists of pain and itching. Cortisone cream, pain medication, or the application of cold may help the pain. Persons with known allergy to stings should carry a sting kit which contains a syringe of epinephrine.

An allergic reaction may start with welts around the bite or elsewhere and progress to respiratory distress that may worsen to the point of death. The onset may be immediate, or it may take several hours. Anytime welts are seen after a sting, assume that an allergic reaction is occurring and evacuate. If a sting kit is available, the epinephrine should be injected.

INSECT BITES

Treatment of bites includes pain medication to ease itch and possibly a cortisone cream. If there is an open wound from the bite or from too much scratching, treat it like other open wounds.

TICKS AND LEECHES

Remove by applying alcohol or insect repellent. Ticks and leeches may also be gently grasped and removed with a firm, steady pull using caution not to crush the body or tear the head off and leave it in the skin.

POISONOUS PLANTS

POISON IVY, OAK AND SUMAC

All three cause areas of small watery blisters with pain and itching. Treat with pain medication and possibly an antihistamine. Cool compresses can also ease the pain and itch. Cortisone cream may also be useful.

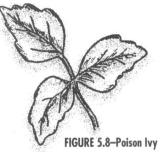

FIGURE 5.8–Poison Ivy

The Camper's Pocket Handbook

The tiny stinging hairs of the underside of the leaves cause severe irritation with pain and itching. Apply insect repellent that has a high DEET concentration to relieve the irritation. Pain medication may also be used.

FIGURE 5.9–Stinging Nettle

Broken Bones

A broken bone (a fracture) causes acute pain, especially when gentle pressure is applied at the site of the break. Deformity is common as is bruising and shortening of the affected limb. It may be impossible to tell whether a bone is broken or just sprained. When in doubt, treat it as a break. Suspected broken bones should be immobilized in the position in which they are found.

SPLINTING BROKEN BONES

Splints may be made from sticks, bark slabs, ski poles, foam pads, canoe paddles, backpack frames, or any other firm, supportive material. The splint must immobilize both the joint above and the joint below the break. Add padding to fit deformities. Do not manipulate the injured part to fit the splint.

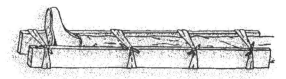

FIGURE 5.10–Leg Splint

Fractures of the shoulder, collar bone, upper arm, forearm, wrist, and hand may all be immobilized with a "sling and swathe," possibly in conjunction with a splint on the upper arm or forearm. The sling supports the lower arm while the swathe secures both the upper and lower arm to the chest. The chest serves as the splint to which the injured arm is secured.

A broken finger may be splinted by taping it to the next finger with padding between them. A broken toe may be taped to the toe next to it.

SPRAINS & STRAINS

Sprains and strains from over-extending, stretching, or twisting may be impossible to distinguish from a broken bone. Pain and swelling are immediate, as is decreased ability to move or bear weight on the affected joint.

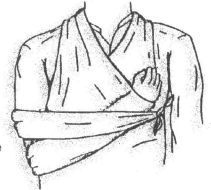

FIGURE 5.11– Sling and Swathe

Immobilize, elevate, and apply cold for 20 minutes at a time, at least 4 times a day for several days. Do not allow the patient to bear weight or use the injured part if doing so causes pain.

FEVER

Fever may be treated with aspirin or acetaminophen and by increasing fluid intake. Severe fever, in excess of 105 degrees, should be aggressively treated by externally cooling the patient with water.

CONSTIPATION

Three days with no bowel movement should cause concern. Increase fluid intake and eat fruits. At breakfast, eat a combination of a hot beverage and cold food or vice-versa to help stimulate the bowels. After 5 days with no bowel movement, a laxative may be necessary. Use as directed and expect abdominal cramping and possible diarrhea.

DIARRHEA

Diarrhea that follows a few days of constipation is seldom serious and usually lasts less than 24 hours. Viral diarrhea also usually lasts only 24 hours but may go on for several days with stools gradually becoming fewer. Treat with rest and fluid replacement.

If diarrhea lasts more than a few days, if there is fever over 100 degrees, or blood in the stools, a more serious infection is possible. Whatever the cause, an antibiotic will be needed and evacuation is necessary.

VOMITING

Seek and treat the underlying cause such as altitude sickness, contaminated food or water, exhaustion, etc. Treat with rest and fluids as tolerated. Avoid solid foods.

The Camper's Pocket Handbook

APPENDICITIS

Symptoms usually start with a general discomfort in the area of the navel and a low fever. Over a few hours, the discomfort develops into pain and moves toward the right lower quadrant of the abdomen. Do not give a laxative.

If the abdomen is rigid or if the patient feels very severe pain when gentle pressure applied on the abdomen is suddenly released, the patient should be evacuated.

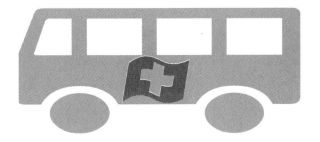

6

EVACUATION & RESCUE

"The Best Laid Plans ..."

L ife in the backcountry is not immune to "Murphy's Law." It is possible, in spite of your best efforts or because of preventable mistakes, for things to happen that could jeopardize the success or safety of your trip. Regardless of exactly what caused the situation, it is likely that if you are in trouble, you are either lost, unable to travel, missing valuable equipment, or you or a member of your party are too ill or injured to continue safely.

STOP AND THINK

The first step is to stop and take stock of your situation. Start taking notes right away. Keep a regular record of how the situation is changing, what decisions you make and what problems come up. Clearly look at your resources as well as your problems. Make a careful inventory of everything that you have with you. Include your clothing and all the things in your pockets. Think about each item and what you may be able to use it for or what you may be able to improvise with it.

Now, think about what you are likely to face as you do what you must to deal with your situation. Anticipate that conditions may get worse, people will become tired and discouraged, and that it may take quite some time for things to get better. But make up your mind to survive! You can make it!

Consider all the skills, talents and weaknesses of each person and assess what each one may be able to do or not do. At this point, it's important to keep everyone busy with specific tasks. Doing calm, routine chores does wonders to ease panic and fear. Don't discuss or worry about who or what is to blame for your situation. That won't do you any good now. Your emphasis must be to decide on a course of action that will improve your situation. Whatever action you decide to take, do it. Be sure to identify in advance at what point you will try something different if the first choice does not work. Then, don't vary from your plan.

LOST

If you're lost, admit it out loud. It will help you accept the fact and begin to think constructively about what to do next. Then sit down, rest, and eat a little. From here on out, your highest priorities must be conserving energy, obtaining shelter and water, and signaling for help.

In order to be found, you must be where a searcher can see you. If at all possible, travel to a nearby open area where you can be seen from the air. Open hilltops, meadows, beaches, and river banks are good choices. Don't go any further than you have to. As you travel, you may be moving farther away from where searchers expect you to be.

Find a shelter or build one as best you can. (See **"EMERGENCY SHELTERS"** in Chapter 1.) Then, find water. Don't worry about looking for food now. You can survive many days without eating, but you must have water and shelter very soon.

Once you have shelter and water, start work on signaling for help. Stay calm. Work slowly and deliberately to conserve your energy and reduce the risk of getting hurt.

EVACUATION

When you're faced with a situation in which you or a member of your party is ill or injured, there are generally three choices to consider.

CONTINUE THE TRIP

Continuing the trip is possible only if the patient can travel without making his condition worse or jeopardizing others. On a rugged trip, each person must be able to pull his or her own weight at all times. If the others must slow the pace or share the work for one who is ill or injured, the entire group loses its ability to cope with the unexpected and may be at a greater risk for more serious problems. An alternative may be to continue to an early stopping point or turn around and go back.

STAY IN PLACE & SEND FOR HELP

Staying in place and sending someone out for help may bring faster rescue, but only if the time travel to help is less than the time for activation of rescue that will happen when you fail to return from the wild at the expected time. At least one person must stay with the patient. Two strong travelers should be sent out for help. If only one is available, reconsider the risks of him traveling alone versus the safety of waiting to be found. The time saved may not be worth the risk.

The travelers should be sent with detailed written

information including explanation of entire situation (dates and times), exact location (send map with spot marked), number and condition of patient(s), treatment provided and needed, supplies or equipment needed, type of evacuation needed, and estimated maximum time that patient can wait.

STAY IN PLACE & WAIT FOR HELP

Staying in place and waiting for help is usually the safest option for all concerned, provided sufficient equipment and provisions are available and no other conditions exist that may jeopardize the group. (It may be necessary to move to a safer location before making camp to await help.)

Waiting for help depends upon your pre-trip notifications and the reliability of the contact person or agency to start rescue when they are not contacted by the deadline date and time. The more information you left with the contact person or agency, the easier and more rapidly they will be able to help.

While you're waiting, protect the patient in the best shelter available. The location of the shelter should be visible by air, such as an open field or along a riverbank. There should also be a clear area nearby for laying out ground-to-air signals and possible helicopter landing.

An immobile patient needs constant care with attention to fluid intake and warmth. Bodily functions may need to be assisted with a makeshift urinal from a wide-mouth bottle. A hole may be cut in the sleeping pad over a small hole in the ground to allow defecation, or a plastic bag can be used.

HELICOPTER RESCUE

In some situations a helicopter may be necessary to extricate a patient from the wild. Be thoughtful about requesting helicopter evacuation as it is very expensive and the patient may be responsible for paying for the service in some areas. Don't request it unless it's really needed.

Helicopter evacuation is generally possible at elevations up to 10,000 feet, with possible limitations due to weather, visibility, and the need for a safe landing site. A landing site should be a wide area, flat and unobstructed on all sides. A surface of bare rock is best, and a clear field is acceptable. Snow is very poor for helicopters without skis. A minimum of 100 feet in all directions must be clear for most helicopters to land. Most pilots prefer a much larger clear area particularly upwind of the landing site since they usually try to land and take off into the wind.

A signal of some type should be made to indicate

wind direction and speed. A smoky fire downwind of the site or a brightly colored flag of material that is easily visible will work. If it is dark or dusky, additional lighting on the landing surface will be helpful. As the helicopter lands, protect the patient and rescuers from flying debris and dust. Don't approach the helicopter until directed to do so by the pilot! When you approach, do so only toward the front of the helicopter. Keep looking at the pilot as you approach. When moving away from the helicopter, go away from the front of it also, so the pilot can see you. Due to the extreme danger of the tail rotor, stay completely away from the tail areas of the helicopter. If on a slope approach from the downhill side.

GROUND-TO-AIR-SIGNALS

The first contact with help is frequently a visual sighting by an airplane or helicopter. The basic signal of distress is 3 of almost any type of alerting device. Whether it is 3 shots fired, 3 whistle blasts, or 3 smoky campfires in a triangle or row, the message to a pilot or rescuer will be that help is needed quickly. If you are using fires as signals, it's best to prepare the fires in advance and wait to light them until you see an aircraft.

Other signals may be fashioned on the ground with a variety of bright objects such as sleeping

The Camper's Pocket Handbook

bags, parkas, tarps, etc. Whatever material used should contrast sharply with the ground and, if possible, be piled high enough to cast a shadow which will emphasize visibility from the air. The size of any visual signals should be considerably larger than seems necessary. Figures on the ground should be at least 8 to 10 feet long.

HAND SIGNALS

When you have been spotted by a plane or helicopter, wave to it by holding **BOTH HANDS** over your head to indicate you need help. Waving one hand usually indicates "I'm OK."

FLARES AND SMOKE SIGNALS

Aerial flares and smoke signals are useful, but they should not be wasted. Wait until the search plane is heard and preferably seen before firing one. A smoke signal may be used to show wind direction for a landing helicopter. Flares and smoke signals may start fires if they fall on combustible material. Fire them over water if possible.

SIGNAL MIRROR

A signal mirror is effective when there is at least some sunshine to work with and the sun is above and/or generally in front of the signaler when facing the target. A mirror made for signaling generally has an opening in the center to sight through. With this type mirror, look through the opening at a nearby surface and adjust the angle until a bright spot is seen. The spot indicates exactly where the signal is shining. The mirror is then adjusted to flash across the target.

A regular small mirror can also be used for signaling. Hold the mirror so it shines on your outstretched hand. Face the target and hold your outstretched hand so the target is seen over the hand. Move the mirror so the light shines on your hand. Then tilt the mirror to flash the light just over your hand, directly at the target. An improvised mirror may be made from nearly any shiny object or material such as aluminum foil.

Mirror flashes may be seen for many miles, even in very hazy weather. Keep shining the mirror across the horizon even if no plane or boat is seen.

CAMPFIRE READINGS

The Valley of the Blue Mist

As Told by Doc Forgey

About a hundred years ago there were three boys who decided that they would go to the gold fields in California and try to strike it rich. In those days, youngsters very often left home at an early age. The discovery of gold in California could mean wealth, perhaps more important, a chance for adventure and to leave hard and drab work in the East.

These three youngsters decided to band together—after all, they had known each other all the way through grade school. They liked and trusted each other, and had helped one another often before. It was a dangerous long journey. They took the money that they had and were able to buy passage on an ocean-going ship that would sail around Cape Horn off South America. They arrived in San Francisco and from there they headed to the gold fields.

Well, they were late in arriving. When the news of gold spreads, it spreads fast. Adventurers from all over the United States, from the Orient, from around the world had made the trek to California.

As they traveled to ateas where the latest rumors told of great finds, they did so as part of a large, milling mob of eager gold seekers. Life was expensive. This was the frontier and everything had to be brought in from small communities that were not large enough to support such demands on their farms and craftsmen. Local farmers and workers had frequently deserted their work and had joined the gold seekers.

But a living could be scratched out, and who could tell, but anyone might strike it rich by finding a mother lode. So they joined the crowds and kept working the placer deposit, finding a little color (as gold was called when mixed with the stream gravel). Placer deposits are hard work. Gold which has been washed down from the hills by the rivers is mixed with the stream gravel. By scooping up pans full of this mixture and washing the lighter stones away from the heavier gold, the prospectors could separate the valuable gold dust and nuggets.

But the goal was to find a Mother Lode—the source of the placer gold. Prospectors always tried to follow the grains of gold up the river beds, hoping they would be led to the vein of gold from whence these nuggets were cut and carried by the water. Then, instead of washing and washing for more specks of gold, they would have a solid vein of pure gold to cut away from the surrounding rock! They would have wealth beyond their wildest dreams!

One day the three boys came upon a river that only had a few miners working the placer deposits near a fairly large, but abandoned tent camp. They thought that there wouldn't be much gold there, otherwise there would be more miners. But when they started to pan, they found some of the best gold that they had come across! They were excited! By working this stream they could make a fortune if the gold held up!

Soon dusk approached. They joined the few other prospectors at the tent camp to cook supper and were invited to stay in an abandoned tent. They were amazed at how rich this stream was, and yet how few miners were working there.

An old man told them, "You need not be surprised boys. You may not be here long either. There are things more important than gold! But whatever you do as long as you stay in this valley, get into the tents by nightfall. Don't get caught in the valley in the blue mist. People die who get caught by it. It carries some sickness, but we have survived it. Do as we do, get into your tent before the blue mist comes down the valley!"

And that night, the blue mist again came. At first fingers of thick blue fog rolled down the valley and curled around the tents. It was dark, about 10:00 P.M., and the lantern cast an eerie glow with the fog lapping higher and higher on the tents, until finally all was obscured.

The three friends were safe in a tent, hardly believing what the old timers had told them, but not wishing to dare their luck either. Day after day they worked the riches of this stream; night after night they sought refuge in the tents as the blue mist slid down the river from higher in the valley, obscuring everything and bringing all activity outside the camp to a stop.

And as they would work on any other river, by day they panned further and further upstream, looking for richer color, looking for a concentration of gold that might mean that they were nearing the Mother Lode. But they always made sure to heed the old man's advice to be back in the tent camp by night-fall, long before the fingers of blue mist curled down the valley.

One day they spotted an abandoned

cabin, high in the valley. Its door was unlocked and upon checking it out they found it fully furnished, apparently abandoned by the owner. That night they asked the ole timers about this cabin, so conveniently located high in the valley closer to the richer source of placer deposits which they had worked their way to.

"Stay in the cabin by day, if you must. But whatever you do, get back to this camp by night-fall. Don't let your greed cause you to get caught you there over night. That cabin wasn't abandoned—the owner was Bill Murphy, who some say was the first prospector in this valley. He died in that cabin, and by the way they found him it was a horrible death. The same horrible death that kills anyone caught by the blue mist."

More than that the old timers couldn't tell them. But they were obviously afraid for their lives. The valley and its blue mist was holding some terrible secret and these old men would be of no help in solving the mystery. . . .

Mike, one of the three boys, finally had enough of the long trek back down to the tent camp, especially when there was a fully equipped cabin so close to their diggings. He announced one day that he was spending the night in the cabin. That morning he took his bedding, several days of his rations, and packed them along to the diggings. Tom and Roy tried to talk him out of it.

"Why take the chance?" Tom asked. "We have it OK at the tent camp. We are making good money. And it's obvious something terrible has happened in this valley. Those old miners aren't afraid of anything, except the blue mist. Let's just stay together and forget that cabin."

Mike wouldn't hear of it. He worked with them during the day, but that night Tom and

Roy had to return to the tent camp without him. And as the night wore on, they anxiously awaited the coming of the mist.

About 10:00 P.M., as usual, the fingers of thick, blue mist curled through the tent camp—soon obscuring the view of the twinkling light from the cabin up the valley. Finally, about 1:00 A.M. they heard something—they thought—way up the valley, possibly from the cabin. Tom couldn't believe that they had let Mike stay up there alone.

"We promised each other that we would stick together, no matter what," he reminded Roy. The old prospectors were furious that they had let Mike stay up there, for they had learned to like these three boys from the East. They didn't want anything to happen to them, and here they had gone and challenged the deadly blue mist.

But morning finally did come and they

left as soon as the sun shined into the valley over the mountains, burning off the blue mist and sending light into the dark valley.

When they got to the cabin, they couldn't believe their eyes! Mike was dead. And worse, the cabin door was open and he lay half out of the door with a look of terror frozen on his face. A fear that struck the others right to the heart. The old men said that they had enough, they were leaving this valley for help. It wasn't safe to stay any longer, no matter how much gold was there.

Roy and Tom were stunned! And sick at their loss. And mad that they had not helped their friend as they had promised when they set out from home together.

In a daze they returned to the now abandoned tent camp after burying their friend near the cabin. They had to decide what to do. Should they return home to tell Mike's parents? They had enough money to return home, but not enough to buy a farm or start a business if they returned now to the East. But more than that, they mourned their friend. This mourning turned to anger and frustration. Tom finally told Roy that they could not leave until they had done something to solve the mystery of their friend's death. They could not go home without being able to tell Mike's parents what had actually happened. Some beast or some person must be responsible for this, and whoever—or whatever—it must be punished.

Tom could think of only one way to do this. They must return to the cabin, armed, and spend the night. That way they could solve the mystery of the Valley of the blue mist!

Roy was horrified! No way was he going to spend the night in that cabin! He thought the idea was crazy and he told Tom so in no uncertain terms. Tom was rigid in his plan.

He felt that it was their duty as they had abandoned their friend—they owed this to him.

Roy could not talk him out of it. But there was no way that HE would go up that valley and spend the night in the blue mist. As evening approached, the boys each had their mind made up. Tom packed his gear, including their only rifle, and headed up the valley to the cabin. It was already late when he left, and he had to hurry to beat the blue mist.

When he got there he made sure that the door was latched and windows shut. He moved the heavy table in front of the door, and to help support it, also slid the heavy chest of drawers against it.

Down in the valley Roy was alone in the tent camp. The old timers had left in a hurry, not even taking their equipment. An old clock ticked on as night fell. He realized

The Camper's Pocket Handbook

what a terrible error he had made. His friend was trapped at the cabin, he was alone in this dreadful valley. Just two nights ago he had been with the two best friends he ever had—without a care in the world. Now he was exhausted, alone without a rifle, and his remaining friend was at the head of the valley that was full of death and mystery.

The minutes on the old wind up clock ticked by. A proud possession of one of the miners, it had been left behind in the hasty abandonment of the camp. Soon it was 10:00 P.M.; the fingers of mist again curled through the silent camp. Terror struck—he waited and listened. He could hear nothing. The swirling mist climbed higher and soon obscured all view of the stars and the other tents. He was utterly alone. Oh, how he wished he had stuck with Tom in the cabin—or wherever he wanted to go. After all, Tom was his best friend and might even now be needing his help. And how about him—alone and without a gun in abandoned tents—alone in a thick, swirling mist.

The night lasted and lasted, as night full of terror always do. Soon the glow of the sun penetrated the thick fog, and the mist started lifting from the valley.

Roy scrambled up the valley to the cabin. From the river's edge he shouted for Tom—but there was no answer from the cabin! He climbed up the path . . .

AAAUUUGGGHH! THERE AT THE FRONT OF THE CABIN—THE DOOR OPENED, WAS HIS FRIEND'S BODY! Twisted in an agony of death, the table and dresser knocked over, the rifle off to one side. The rifle had not even been fired! What could possibly have caught brave Tom so suddenly that he couldn't even get a shot off!

Roy knew what he had to do. He could

not return home now, he had to find out what mystery the Blue Mist held. He had to avenge his friends' deaths! Oh, how he wished he had stayed with Tom. How could he have been so stupid to have let him stay in this cabin alone, but now he had to make all of that up to both of his friends.

He immediately returned to the tent camp. There he got nails and a hammer. He brought extra kerosene for the lantern and two extra lanterns. He brought rope and some old, empty cans. He would return to that cabin and avenge the death of his friends, come what may!

Weighted down with his supplies, he took a last look at the now abandoned tent camp. He trudged up the now familiar stream bed that he and his friends had worked together for so long.

At the cabin he noted that the old clock, which his friends had started was still ticking, and the time seemed correct. He took nails and went to work on the windows, boarding them up—nailing them soundly shut. Nothing could possibly get in. He strung the empty cans on the rope around the cabin, so he should hear anyone, or anything approach. He raked the dirt so that he could see any foot prints the next day. Finally, everything outside seemed ready. He shut the door of the cabin for the last time, and firmly nailed it shut.

He moved the dresser in front of the door. Thinking to further barricade it, he tried to move the large trunk located along one wall of the cabin. The trunk was incredibly heavy, too heavy to move. Opening it he found only a layer of old clothes, a belt, and a few odd items. The trunk had been nailed to the floor. Leaving it there, he filled the kerosene lanterns. He made sure the rifle was loaded, and then started the long wait for night.

Night comes suddenly in the mountains. When the sun finally lowers towards the horizon, it will suddenly dip behind a mountain top and be quickly lost from view. Shadows appear immediately and soon thereafter it is night.

With night in this valley comes more than darkness. The dreaded blue mist starts forming the chasms and rivulets that form the valley on the mountain side. As Roy waited, he watched the clock. Soon it was 10:00 P.M., and the mist started swirling beyond the cabin door, filling the basin of the river and sliding its way down to the abandoned tent camp. Fingers of mist slid between now empty tents.

At the cabin Roy continued to wait. His heart pounding, he thought of his friends and he thought of his own danger. The night deepened and outside the mist covered the cabin. He listened intently for any sound amongst the tin cans outside, any evidence of movement from the nearby forest.

And finally he DID hear something. At first it was a quiet whisper. Then, more of a hiss. It sounded close, very close to the cabin. Could it be a snake? Or a whole coil of snakes? Surely there would have been some sign earlier when the others had been killed.

The hiss was close, near the window, SUDDENLY HE FELT A TIGHT CONSTRICTION GRABBING AT HIS THROAT. He thought he was losing his sight, the cabin was becoming darker! No! It was the kerosene lights, they were flickering out!

AAAUUUGGGHHH!

VIOLENT SPASMS TWITCHED HIS BODY, HE GASPED FOR AIR, HE STRUGGLED TO ESCAPE! He couldn't breathe! The light from the lamps was out, the hissing, more of a sighing was louder now. Its location was easy to identify—IT WAS COMING FROM THE EMPTY TRUNK!

He grabbed at the dresser and threw it aside. The planks! He ripped at the planks, the spasm racking his body!

Early the next day a column of men proceeded up the valley. It was the group of old miners, leading a posse from the nearest town. Upon finding the cabin sealed shut, they took their pikes to the door and smashed their way through. Inside they found the contorted body of the last of the three friends.

These men decided that they would take matters into their own hands. Furiously they would destroy this cabin where so many had died. They started tearing it apart, board by board. When they reached the flooring, they too noted the old trunk nailed to the floor. Breaking it apart, they made an incredible discovery. The trunk apparently had a secret, false bottom. It covered a shaft leading into a hidden mine. And that mine proved to be the Mother Lode! Rather than claiming this rich vein of ore for what it was, the miner had simply staked a claim and built his cabin over the spot. Then he concealed the shaft opening with the trunk, a much better concealment than a trap door under a rug in the cabin. But unknown to the old miner, he eventually reached a pocket of deadly gas within his mine. When night fell in the valley, the barometric pressure dropped. On the outside this caused the blue mist to rise up from the ground. But inside the cabin, it allowed the mine shaft to start blowing air out its opening, just as a cave entrance will do when the pressure is right. But this mine was laced with deadly cyanide gas, which, when it caught its victim, racked them with spasm and a very quick death.

This mine eventually became known as the Empress Mine, one of the richest finds of the gold fields. But a mine with a tragic beginning, one that killed three good friends in the midst of their life of adventure together.

"The Valley of the Blue Mist" was taken from **Campfire Stories … Things That Go Bump in the Night** by William Forgey, M.D. Copyright © 1985. **Published by ICS Books, The Globe Pequot Press, P.O. Box 833, Old Saybrook, CT 06475.** *To order call 800-243-0495*

INDEX